MILLION
DOLLAR
MAVERICK

MILLION DOLLAR MAVERICK

*Forge Your Own Path
to Think Differently,
Act Decisively, and
Succeed Quickly*

ALAN WEISS

AUTHOR OF
MILLION DOLLAR CONSULTING

bibliomotion inc.

First published by Bibliomotion, Inc.
39 Harvard Street
Brookline, MA 02445
Tel: 617-934-2427
www.bibliomotion.com

Printed in the United States of America

Library of Congress Cataloging-in-Publication Data

Names: Weiss, Alan, 1946- author.
Title: Million dollar maverick : forge your own path to think differently,
    act decisively, and succeed quickly / Alan Weiss.
Description: Brookline, MA : Bibliomotion, [2016]
Identifiers: LCCN 2015050643| ISBN 9781629561264 (hardback) | ISBN
    9781629561288 (enhanced ebook)
Subjects: LCSH: Success in business. | Creative ability in business. |
    Entrepreneurship. | Strategic planning. | Management. | BISAC: BUSINESS &
    ECONOMICS / Consulting. | BUSINESS & ECONOMICS / Entrepreneurship. |
    BUSINESS & ECONOMICS / Motivational.
Classification: LCC HF5386 .W377 2016 | DDC 658.4/09—dc23
LC record available at http://lccn.loc.gov/2015050643

This is for Maria, Danielle, Jason, John, Grace, Gabrielle, Alaina, Buddy, and Bentley. There's nothing so strong as family.

Acknowledgments

My life was hugely formed by my grammar school teachers, who taught in an age when discipline was expected, parents didn't protect their children from it, and rules were important. They have influenced me more than my high school, undergraduate, and graduate instructors combined, an undiminished influence still present over half a century later.

Thank you: Mrs. Grothousen, Mrs. Stephanour, Mrs. Fleming, Miss Mandelkern, Mrs. Bowman, Mrs. O'Brien, Mr. Heitman, Mrs. Johnson, Mrs. Lippert, and Miss Baratini.

Thanks to Barry Banther and his colleagues in the Elite Retreat I facilitate annually for suggesting the theme of this book. It had never occurred to me, an example of the benefits of surrounding yourself with smart people.

And thanks for Erika and Jill here at Bibliomotion, a publishing house that treats authors as friends, a novel concept!

Contents

- How to become a singular presence
- The benefits of contrarianism
- Taking comfort in being different
- Why the "in crowd" is the wrong crowd

This is the expressway to being comfortably different and uncomfortably contrarian: comfort the afflicted and afflict the comfortable. The "black hole" of convention entraps too many people in a gravity of failure they can't escape.

- The good thing about being broke
- Failure is seldom fatal
- Resilience and ego
- Evaluating upside/downside

The best people I have met have been broke, sometimes more than once. They have a perspective and appreciation that feed their passion and inform their direction. I'm not insisting you lose all your money first, but I am suggesting that you must create resilience if you're going to create success.

Chapter 3 Gaining Influence   33

- Treat others as they expect to be treated
- Getting there "firstest with the mostest"
- How to compromise and do it your way
- The power of the calming voice

Too many people ease up around the turns in life. Life isn't a marathon but a constant series of sprints. Speed is as important as content—I know that's heresy—but we live in a world of instant gratification, where instant response usually carries the day.

Chapter 4 Critical Thinking Skills   49

- How to create your own system of success
- Finding cause, not blame
- Identifying distinctions
- If nothing changes, nothing happens

Consciousness is a factor of how fast we process information. A dog has a higher consciousness than a rabbit, but many people have higher consciousness levels than other people. These are learnable skills, based on asking the right questions to generate the right answers. Most people are asking the wrong questions.

Chapter 5 Learning the Hard Way   67

- We should all be fired
- Not all relationships are made in heaven
- Throwing water on personal outrage
- Self-esteem must be built daily

Self-esteem, and lack thereof, is the monster under the bed. You can hear it in people's self-talk: "I shouldn't," "They'll question me," "It's not my place," "They'll never listen to me." The creation of high self-esteem is a remedial skill, and one I've helped thousands to accomplish—and they thrive as a result.

My early "success" involved shooting everyone in the room, then asking if they could support my position. Then I learned that there was always someone with heavier artillery and allies were the key to success. We need to understand and apply the principles of leveraged support and convincing others that "the road less traveled" is less traveled because it's an inferior road.

We can stage-manage and choreograph our careers. I was a "prisoner" working in some firms, but I also found that many people who are refugees from corporations and start their own entrepreneurial companies are now working for a tougher boss! We are able to shape our own lives and businesses, our relationships and interactions. Our choice is to learn the steps or simply follow while someone else leads—not much of a choice.

Chapter 8 The Word 117

- Communicating at the speed of light
- Persuading through metaphor and example
- Translating and reframing
- Owning transactions

Many people scoff at language "purists" and insist that vernacular must prevail. Yet every business today is a communications business first and foremost, and the best of them craft very clear messages and establish very tangible positions. There is no more powerful tool (or weapon) than words used with intent, purpose, and agility. Individuals and companies can rise above the "lowest common denominator" approach and dominate their markets. When I began speaking for money, I thought my common-sense approach would get me tossed out. What it got me was return engagements and high income.

Chapter 9 The "App" of Success 133

- Attracting people who attract people
- The power of community
- The gravitas of true exceptionalism
- Your personal GPS

The iPhone "app" intrigued me because it resembled a perpetual motion attraction machine (more phones, more apps, more apps, more phones, upsell apps, etc.). I duplicated this approach in customer communities, with highly respected clients drawing more and more highly respected clients in a nonstop boom of marketing gravity and gravitas. Our real value is often most represented by the company we keep.

Chapter 10 No Guilt, No Fear, No Peer 151

- The four levels of existence
- How to seal the watertight doors
- Moving from a poverty to an abundance mentality
- Your personal journey

There Is Always a Bigger Boat (TIAABB). The point is to find comfort in one's own skin while moving from a poverty mentality toward an abundance mentality (as has been the flow of this book). To achieve this, we must consciously change relationships, beliefs, interests, and even values—and seal the "watertight doors" behind us so that we don't revert. (Have you seen successful people who never reach for the check or who become paralyzed when faced with a needed purchase?) We need a mantra of "life, contribution, and success."

Epilogue The Liberal Artist 173

How to reclaim what has been denied us in our education and experiences in a world of conformity, rewards for "showing up," and lower common denominators.

Appendix 181

References 183

Index 185

Introduction

I'm told this is my sixtieth book, counting foreign translations and revised editions. Who would have thought?

I'm a guy originally from modest means who quite simply looked at the wealth and opportunity available in this country as brilliant opportunity, since the only place I had to go was up! I never despaired; I always thought I had a chance. I knew I wouldn't win every contest, but I also knew I had no chance of winning if I didn't enter the contest, both literally and metaphorically, physically and emotionally.

In the 1950s I would sit on the floor in the entry to the bathrooms in public school with my jacket over my head. This wasn't a game, it was an air raid drill, and the bricks and mortar around me and cheap fabric over my head were supposed to protect me from the blasts and radiation of atomic bombs, should they rain down on Manhattan, a mile across the Hudson River.

I was in high school during the Cuban Missile Crisis, and I remember women crying in the hallways. Since those days, terrorism, Ebola, tsunamis, nuclear plant leaks, and MERS have all seemed serious, but never as terrifying. *One thing age provides is a glorious perspective.*

I've spent most of my lifetime trying to help others. As I write this I have a global community of entrepreneurs who participate—in person and virtually—in myriad experiences under my auspices throughout the year, and often daily. I've coached thousands of entrepreneurs and thousands of business executives, consulting with the some of the largest firms on the planet, and have worked with governors and the military, celebrities and authors, beauty queens and tech geniuses. My travels and work have taken me to more than sixty countries. I've been lost in the Norwegian woods, accosted with a machine gun in Argentina, flown in airplanes hit by lightning on five different occasions, and piloted a WWII B-24 bomber and the Goodyear Blimp.

You get the idea—I've seen a lot. My wife told me an autobiography would be self-indulgent, and I've been married to her for forty-seven years, so you have to think she's right about that. But my friends and publisher convinced me that a memoir covering what I've learned and how I've applied it to create great success and a wondrous life would be a book worth writing.

It appears they're right—I have a thousand advance orders before I've even finished the introduction, which isn't bad. Of course, my wife isn't one of them. But then again, she's seen it herself.

I'm hoping this is the opportunity for you to see it, too.

Alan Weiss
East Greenwich, Rhode Island

CHAPTER 1

Leaving the Herd: Why the Lone Wolf Succeeds More Than the Lone Calf

This is the expressway to being comfortably different and uncomfortably contrarian: comfort the afflicted and afflict the comfortable. The "black hole" of convention entraps too many people in a gravity of failure they can't escape.

How to Become a Singular Presence

It was Bizarro World. Seventeen teachers sat in classroom seats while four students took turns lecturing to them. Unlike most classrooms in Emerson High School, the occupants in this one were paying rapt attention during the five minutes allotted each speaker. The eye contact was intense enough to require sunscreen.

This thirty-minute meeting was the complete audition and final vote for the first (and only) exchange student that Emerson would ever produce. The year was 1963, and an entrepreneurial local newspaper reporter had arranged for a Finnish student he had met to spend a half-year in each of the public high schools in Union City, New Jersey, a poor city, at the time the most densely populated city in the United States (fifty thousand people in about two square miles).

The "committee of seventeen" had chosen four nominees to be the return student (who would spend six weeks touring Europe, ending in Finland over the summer, since none of us was about to learn Finnish). They chose the quarterback and captain of the football team; the president of the yearbook; the president of the class; and me, the president of the student council and editor-in-chief of the school newspaper. We were apprised of the selections (back then no one argued about fairness or gender) and asked if we would accept if chosen, our parents were consulted, and then we were told to prepare to answer a question in front of the committee. The five-minute interview would determine, by immediate majority vote thereafter, who would have his life incredibly changed.

It was the height of the Cold War, and the question was this: How would you defend the United States to people you meet in Europe when you're asked about our foreign policy?

I had luck and pluck. Luck because my last name starts with "W," and I was to be last in the alphabetic order. But here's the pluck. I had an inkling that this trip would have a profound change on my life, and I knew we could not just afford any college. I also knew that my hometown of Union City—the "embroidery capital of the world" proclaimed the city's sign as you shot by on the way to the Lincoln Tunnel and New York—held no future for me. I decided that I couldn't risk simply giving a better but similar answer to the others.

I had to give a completely different answer to truly stand out from everybody else. My turn was approaching.

"I wouldn't defend the United States," I told the room of suddenly bolt-upright teachers. "I would explain who we are and how we're more similar to their own country than dissimilar." I went on from there.

All the way to Europe.

In those five minutes, my life was changed. I sailed on the original *Queen Mary*, visited nine countries, took my first airplane rides, met with the U.S. general who commanded our Berlin forces, and even dated a future Miss Finland.* My life changed from black and white to Technicolor. All because I decided that I had better stand out in a crowd, and I understood that I had a better chance of standing out not merely by being better, but by being *different*.

We are inculcated from youth to blend in, to be one of the crowd, to be accepted. This has a chilling effect later in our lives, as characterized by the "ticky-tacky" houses made famous in Malvina Reynolds's 1960s' song satirizing conformist attitudes. Normative pressure is monstrous. We point out the odd duck, scorn the free spirit, and chastise the rebel while we struggle to keep abreast of the latest lingo (as I write this it's "bae"—before anyone else), clothing (no matter how uncomfortable), clubs, cars, and furnishings.

There is significant and conclusive research today that we tend to live where people like us live, and join what they join, and act like they act. We are not conformists at birth, but we have "sameness" drilled into us, as we saw in the frenzy to purchase baby clothes identical to those that Kate, Duchess of Cambridge, used to dress her first child, George.

We must resist this ominous gravity, even to "royal" taste.

My observations of both entrepreneurs and successful corporate executives, as well as groundbreaking organizations, are that they don't march to the beat of a distant drummer; they create their uniquely personal music. Here are some examples:

- The U.S. Marine Corps' branding ("a few good men"), which accentuated selectivity, scarcity, and high status for enlistment
- BMW's "ultimate driving machine" slogan, when safety and economy were being touted by others

---

* The last time I was in contact with my Finnish counterpart a few years ago, he was Finland's ambassador to France.

- Apple's emphasis on design, which subordinated engineering and promoted aesthetics as being important in hardware
- Certain dog breeders' choice to specialize solely in white German shepherds, which old-school dog snobs consider a freak caused by recessive genes, but which are now immensely popular with the public (as an independent breed, white shepherds would be in the top quartile)
- Rod Stewart's move from rock to standards, with a voice barely up to it but a passion that's unmistakable, creating an entirely new following (my wife being a devotee)

How does comfort with "being different" help us in our work? Here's how I used my exchange student experience to gain a $250,000 project at a major life insurer.

Mindsets: It's not the "road most traveled or less traveled." It's the road you create for yourself.

Case Study

An executive vice president of a major insurer, which had just gulped down a company almost equal in size, was interviewing six consultants for a "strategic communications project." His concern was that performance would suffer while people were worrying about their jobs and status.

I sat in the reception area as four of the other consulting firms marched in with laptops and PowerPoint presentations. We had drawn lots for presentation order. I was the only solo consultant there. One of the senior managers had read a couple of my books.

When I was called in, I sat down with just my calendar in front of me. The executive was across from me, and a dozen minions surrounded us. Everyone looked exhausted. Cups with cold coffee sat like sentries all over the room. It was *Mad Men* without cigarettes.

"What would you create to calm people and assure they were focused on their jobs?" asked the client. "Give us an idea of what you would tell them and when, and by what means." He sat back and placed his hands behind his head.

"I wouldn't tell them anything," I said.

He sat back up. So did everyone else.

"What was that again?"

"Do you know which offices you're closing?"

"No, a committee is working on that."

"Do you know which officers will remain to head which departments?"

"No, the board has a retreat scheduled to decide that."

"Do you know which company's compensation system will prevail?"

"No, our accounting firm is giving us advice."

"You don't know anything, so don't tell them anything. Simply ask for their concerns, questions, and suggestions. Answer the questions you can, acknowledge those you can't answer, and let everyone know what those inquiries are. As you get information, answer what you can reliably respond to. Let people know you're listening, stop worrying about talking."

At least ten seconds elapsed, which felt to me like half a day.

"That is counterintuitive," he said, finally.

"It is," I said, not knowing what else to say.

"Cancel the last presentation," he said to an assistant, and later that day we had worked out a $250,000 project that required a four months' span but only about three actual weeks of my time.

I am absolutely convinced—because I've done it thousands of times—that simply taking a contrarian or "one-off" view is the secret to success. When someone says to you, "We're in California and you live in New York," as an excuse not to hire you, you're probably apt to say, "But there are nonstop flights, I can absorb part of the expense, Skype is a fine alternative, and I'm happy to make extended visits."

Admit it, you do.

What I say is, "That's exactly why you need me."

Then the other person says, "Why is that?" NOTICE: The other person is now engaged not in explaining why you're not a good alternative but rather in trying to understand why you *are* a good alternative! That's when I say: "I bring a different perspective from the East. All of your competitors are using local help and ideas, and they all have cookie-cutter approaches. You need some fresh air. My credentials and experience are not only better, they're different. The expense, which I'm assuming is what's really bothering you, might be an extra $10,000 over the course of the project, but the 5 percent market share increase we're pursuing would mean another $2 million in revenues. I'd say that's a pretty minor issue, right?"

Bill Belichick, the New England Patriots' head coach, who has won four Super Bowls at this writing, has created plays where people eligible to catch a pass are temporarily ineligible (they must report this to the officials, who inform the other team), and those ineligible are temporarily eligible. It, too, is counterintuitive, until you watch a 325-pound tackle (Nate Solder) who never catches passes actually catch one and rumble like a fast freight train over two defenders into the end zone for a touchdown. That's the equivalent to my $250,000 deal. It's counterintuitive.

And it works, because the other guys don't expect it.

The Benefits of Contrarianism

I built my career as a "contrarian" without knowing it, and began a highly effective brand without realizing it. Sometimes it's better to be lucky than good, but it's best to be both.

In 1985 I was fired in the Admirals Club of American Airlines in Chicago's O'Hare Airport by W. Clement Stone, who owned the consulting firm where I had been president for eighteen months. I had moved my family from New Jersey to Rhode Island, and I had very little savings and no prospects. Stone believed that positive mental attitude was responsible for his $450 million wealth, and I tried to explain to him that he had it reversed—he had a positive mental attitude *because he had $450 million in the bank.* If he gave that sum to everyone, we'd *all* have a positive mental attitude!

He didn't like that, and fired me with minimum severance.*

I told my wife I never again wanted to answer to someone who could arbitrarily control my fate, and that I wanted to go out on my own. Bless her, she said, "Screw the mortgage" (but in New Jersey language), "but you had better get serious!"

I looked around and found that quality was king: Juran and Deming, quality circles, Six Sigma, black belts in quality, fishbones and charts, yada yada. I hated this stuff, and the thought of trying to embrace it and make a living at it was anathema. So I decided that I'd go with my natural inclinations and oppose it.

And a contrarian was born.

---

* Stone was an acolyte of Napoleon Hill and *Think and Grow Rich.* Yet Hill was a failure financially and an alcoholic (Stone told me) and had to be rescued by Stone to survive.

Mindsets: People jump on bandwagons careening down hills. It's a public service to show them how to get off, because they invariably crash, since they don't have the brakes of rational risk assessment.

I began writing for a Boston monthly training magazine after I had submitted one story, "Why Quality Circles Don't Work." Once published, readers (primarily human resource denizens) gathered with pitchforks and torches as in a 1930s Frankenstein movie and began marching uphill to kill the monster. I was so abashed by the vicious feedback (did these people *actually* have black belts?) that I apologized to the editor.

"Kid," he said, in Runyonesque manner, "I want you to write a monthly column, I'll pay you $50 an issue."

"But they hated it," I stammered.

"They *read* it," he instructed me.

Hence, "Revolutions" was born, and ran for six years—seventy-two issues—until the publication was sold. In every single edition I disagreed with something:

- Leadership doesn't start at the top; it starts in the middle.
- Team building can't work because you have committees, not teams.
- Commitment is fine, but compliance is often what's needed.
- The more you pursue a "paperless" office, the more paper you'll get.

Today, nearly thirty years later, many people still call me "the contrarian." I'm sometimes introduced that way at my keynote speeches. The brand has clung to me and I'm proud of it.

What does this mean for you, today? Ask yourself the following questions in these categories.

Personal

- Do I have financial goals appropriate for my talent or am I using others' metrics or even my parents' beliefs (which are often based in a poverty or scarcity mentality)?
- Am I settling or selecting in my personal relationships?
- Do I have a healthy selfishness about my time and energy or do I constantly sacrifice for others out of guilt?
- Do I take vacations and engage in relaxation that is uniquely appealing to me or do I go solely where others have gone and do what they recommend?
- Have I made a conscious effort to change friends and colleagues (or at least add to them) as I grow, or do I know the same people I did five years ago?

Professional

- Am I forming new intellectual property and approaches or am I simply derivative, using ideas and products created elsewhere?
- Do I jump on the bandwagon of fads and wind up crashing at the bottom of the hill, or can I recognize a true trend and add value to it?
- Am I telling the same stories and using the same examples I've been using for years, or am I adding and replacing annually?
- Are my markets expanding geographically and demographically, or can people accuse me of the same old, same old?
- Do I create value in video, audio, print, and electronically, or am I a one-trick pony?

Environment

- Have I become a slave to social media, or do I use more sophisticated means for learning and educating?
- Do I use technology to stop reading books or to read even more books?
- Have I moved from a scarcity mentality to an abundance mentality, or am I stuck in the former despite my improved circumstances?
- Am I continuing to grow and ensuring that I do, or have I simply reached a comfortable plateau?
- Am I leaving a legacy or just a trail?

Mindsets: If you think you should conform to your colleagues, you'll never stand out in a crowd. You'll simply be one of the herd.

Whenever I view an event or movement that appears to be gathering strong momentum quickly, I reach for my contrarian glasses. I'm not talking about Pet Rocks and gimmicks to make a few bucks. What's your view on the perspective I have for these phenomena, below?

Multi-level marketing: This is merely a slick way (as is "network marketing") to perpetuate Ponzi schemes, which are illegal, and which always hurt the late entrants because there are never enough new members to make them much in commissions. Oh, I know that these firms all have "products" they sell, like detergents or phone cards or whatever. But capitalism is about adding value to the environment, not merely trying to earn a commission when someone becomes a member.

Financial experts: These folks are little better than racetrack touts. After all, if someone really *did* know the sure-bet horses, he'd simply bet the farm, make a fortune, and retire. Why sell them to you for $20? The same reasoning obtains here: if the financial people really knew the likely best bets, they'd invest, make their fortunes, and move to Palm Beach. Instead, they're trying to take a percentage of your investment, whether they are right or wrong. What's wrong with that picture?* (Bernie Madoff, by the way, combined these first two examples and harmed thousands of people.)

Ice bucket challenges: Everyone was eager to dunk themselves to show support for ALS (Lou Gehrig's disease), but I was wondering how many "dunkers" also contributed. I think a lot of them felt they had "contributed" by getting doused, which isn't really the point. If you had to pay first, then we'd be talking. I thought this was a lot of showboating and maybe not as much about charity as it could have been. (It's like all those colored ribbons on lapels. It's nice to sport one, but what have you really done for the cause? The same holds true for flag pins versus true patriotism.)

Social media marketing: Most of the "experts" in social media marketing have never marketed anything successfully except their "expertise" as social media marketing experts! If you're selling to a corporate buyer, social media mean less than nothing *because the research is overwhelmingly clear: corporate buyers purchase services based on peer referrals*. If you're talking about retail or consumer purchases (e.g., real estate, insurance, cars), you still have a problem because of all the "noise" on the social platforms and the total lack

---

* Why doesn't anyone make *their* fortune by auditing every financial prophet at year-end and showing the results over a three-year period? Why isn't that on *60 Minutes*?

of validation of claims. Most people waste valuable time, energy, and money trying to market on social media sites rather than in traditional venues (speaking, networking, referrals, publishing).

Gifting forward: This atrocious public habit of alerting someone that they'll receive a "gift" from you if they agree to do the same for someone else is egregiously wrong. If you want to provide gifts, do so anonymously, don't ask to be thanked or "obeyed," and, worse, don't demand it on Facebook! This is simply self-absorption, like the guy driving me somewhere who paused to allow another driver to make a left turn in front of him but who was then outraged when the driver didn't wave to thank him. "Did you do that as a courtesy, or did you do that to get thanked?" I asked, "because it makes a huge difference." He grumbled and drove on. What are your motives?

Okay, now a lot of you are outraged, and I did that on purpose. Before you throw the book at the wall, consider the following:

Are you engaged?
Are you emotionally involved?
Do you want to set me straight?
Have you been thinking about supporting and opposing arguments?
Have you considered changing your view?
Have you thought that I just might be right?
Are you somewhat concerned or even threatened?
Do you remember me?

Congratulations (if you're still holding the book)—you've experienced what contrarianism can do!

Here's a terrific exercise: choose a half-dozen major trends or activities or beliefs in your field, and debunk them. You don't have to believe them wholeheartedly, just have some fun casting doubt on them.

If you do this thoroughly, you'll find that many of your positions *are absolutely valid.* I found, once I started to challenge the usefulness of human resources as a function (since it often competed with external consultants), that, indeed, 99 percent of the time the department had become a vestigial corporate organ less useful than an appendix. I began calling HR "hardly relevant." And I was immediately booked to speak at HR conferences, so that people in the profession stopped breathing their own exhaust and started to hear a challenging and threatening dissonant view.

You can challenge your industry's beliefs, too.

Taking Comfort in Being Different

Kermit the Frog sang eloquently about how it isn't easy being green. This isn't a recent phenomenon. Here's E. E. Cummings: "To be nobody-but-yourself—in a world which is doing its best, night and day, to make you everybody else—means to fight the hardest battle which any human being can fight; and never stop fighting."

Most people resist being different because they perceive that it's painful. That is accurate early in our lives, when being in a fraternity or sorority, wearing the right clothes, using the right slang, and being in the right places and in the right company are so extremely important.

But we don't stay teenagers forever. Like hormones, the urge to "belong" ebbs and flows. As adults, we need a different perspective and to take comfort in the act and art of being different, not to take solace in blending in. The examples of the lone wolves who have succeeded and exceeded are plentiful:

- Fred Smith, who started FedEx when everyone mocked his "hub and spoke" system idea

- Jeff Bezos, who recognized that people would buy books online
- Mark Zuckerburg, who transitioned collegiate chatter into online communities
- Bill Walsh, who changed traditional football offenses to feature multiple receivers with plentiful options and for "scripting" his first ten plays
- Richard Pryor, who changed the laws of comedy and fearlessly used race to attract diverse audiences
- Diana Nyad, who swam from Havana to Key West at age sixty-four without benefit of a shark cage
- Barack Obama, who decided to run for president with only two years' experience in the Senate, against entrenched favorite Hillary Clinton, and whose chief experience was as a community organizer in Chicago

These people find comfort in being different and are pained when they can't be different. That's why so many of us are refugees from large organizations. It's why we grow irritated sitting through mandatory meetings, filling out bureaucratic forms, waiting in inefficient lines. No one who is different and enjoys it likes being pushed into the herd.

How glorious it is—and also how painful—to be an exception.
—Alfred de Musset

Why the "In Crowd" Is the Wrong Crowd

How do you extricate yourself from the sticky spiderweb of affiliations, friends, norms, expectations, pedestrian aspirations, and even parental DNA? How many people became dentists not through love of teeth or even an attraction to service, but because dentistry was "in the family"? How many of you have dentists with high-speed drills in your mouth who are really miserable and frustrated?

The suicide rate among professionals is highest among dentists.

How many psychologists who spend forty (fifty-five-minute) hours a week listening to the unending complaints and trials of others are actually miserable themselves? Do you have a therapist who entered the profession—advertently or inadvertently—to attempt to "cure" her own ills?

The suicide rate among professionals is second highest among psychologists. (When I asked the then-president of the American Psychological Association, with whom I served on a board, why that was, he immediately replied: "Because we draw so many already troubled people to the profession.")

The illustration below helps explain the phenomenon:

Figure 1.1: Respect and Affiliation

The ideal positioning occurs just to the right of the vertical line and well above the horizontal line. We are accepted, if not loved, and the respect for our expertise is huge. That's the world of "trusted advisor," with its high retainer, name your own price, and so forth.

Most of us strive for high affiliation irrespective of respect. We'd rather have people like us, rather have them "on our side," rather have them acknowledge we're "with them." However, the most successful entrepreneurs I've ever observed are those who strive for high respect. If you like me, fine, but it's more important that you respect my expertise and my values.

Mindsets: People pay those they respect, but they have lower expectations for the quality of advice from pals.

Feet to the fire, we'd rather have the best doctor available for our knee replacement or heart stent, not the least expensive and not the one with the best bedside manner. Oh, we'd *prefer* a great bedside manner, and be *pleased* by lower fees, but our *critical requirement* is the best possible expertise. The same holds true for consultants, accountants, designers, architects, and myriad others. Most of us are stunned by the reports of Steve Jobs's unhygienic practices, his sullenness, his lack of patience with others, even his reneging on stock option promises. We had assumed that genius entrepreneurs must be nice people. But from Thomas Edison and the Wright brothers to Ted Turner and Richard Branson, this is simply a myth.

On a less globally known basis, we can see people every day who are successful because of their talents and pursuit of respect, not because they are trying to win Miss Congeniality in a beauty contest. (The reality show *Survivor* demonstrated this in the most blatant ways—contestants broke promises, made false alliances, and engaged in double-dealing, anything not to be voted off the island. Status wasn't about popularity; it was tied to respect for someone else's ability to help you stay on the show, no matter how nefarious the tactics.)

I learned long ago that suffering the label of "arrogant," "aloof," and "remote" was a low price to pay for being sought after, naming my own terms, charging what I desired, and standing far apart from the herd. I was never the football star pursued by cheerleaders after the game, but I was able to chart my own course and attract those who had discretion and taste. (My wife and I were high school sweethearts, married for forty-seven years as I write this.)

CHAPTER 2

Losing the Fear of Failure

The best people I have met have been broke, sometimes more than once. They have a perspective and appreciation that feed their passion and inform their direction. I'm not insisting you lose all your money first, but I am suggesting that you must create resilience if you're going to create success.

The Good Thing About Being Broke

My parents used to argue about how to get the money for the next month's rent, which was usually a week past due already. My father had a variety of commission sales jobs (he was actually a Fuller Brush man at one point), and was sometimes "between jobs." The rent on our four-room apartment was $40. We seldom had it.

I often slid the cardboard I'd hoard from my father's laundered shirts into my sneakers to cover the holes in the soles. Sometimes parts of the bottoms would depart from the uppers and flap like a flag in the breeze when I ran. The cardboard would be replaced when it developed holes, which was almost daily.

However, *we were all broke!* We thought we were fine. There was no Internet, no cable, no adjoining wealthy neighborhood to set us straight. (The television's seven channels appeared to be pure fantasy—no one could live like that.) We would snag balls out of the sewers with coat hangers, since we couldn't afford new ones. We snuck into the movie theater's back door, opened by the one kid who entered legally with the money we pooled. Summer vacations meant playing in the schoolyard or in the streets (hence, the balls winding up in the sewers).

All of our families were blue collar, lower class. We didn't begrudge anyone who had more, because we all figured we'd have more *someday*. We didn't know exactly how, but we did know we were inserted into a process called schooling that would help us along.

I didn't take offense, or blame my parents, or bemoan my fate. I accepted the life I lived and figured that when given the chance, I could improve upon it. Our apartment had holes in the cheap rugs, scratches on the furniture, and paint peeling in various places. One day my father killed a rat with a broken toy I had kept around, which, fortunately, had a sharp point.

Mindsets: Don't bemoan your fate; figure out how to change it.

Many years later, when I was managing an international sales force, I had a sign placed on the wall of my office that said, "No Whining!" I would point to the sign when, inevitably, the disillusioned, unhappy salespeople came in and moaned about the inferiority of their territory, lack of company support, or my own ignorance of proper motivational techniques. But I also kept it there for me. When I began to feel down or victimized or taken advantage of, the sign would eventually catch my attention and bring me back to reality.

A great many people have been born on third base and think they hit a triple. These are the offspring of great wealth who somehow misguidedly believe that they are responsible for their own superb circumstances. You can see them running for public office, funding their campaigns with family money, but offering no talent or smarts. You can see them in fancy schools, with great faculty and modern facilities, where they take easy courses or don't bother to graduate at all. You can see them in failed investments and ruined endeavors, because they never had to develop street smarts to achieve their current fortunate position.

We never feared failure because we had no place to fail *to*. The good think about being broke is that you're at the bottom. You can't fear losing things. Transferred to today's environment, it means that you can't possibly enter a buyer's office and leave with less than you entered with. You can't "lose" anything. You may not get the sale, but you'll be no worse off, and probably better off if you bothered to learn something.

Oscar Wilde observed that "we are all in the gutter, but some of us are looking at the stars."*

It all depends on your perspective. If you have the right work ethic, you won't be harmed by coming from affluent circumstances. But if you don't, you're really not at a disadvantage if you can focus on the stars while you get out of the gutter.

Failure Is Seldom Fatal

Although the quote has been attributed to many, most of us believe it was Winston Churchill who pointed out that "failure is seldom fatal, and success never final—it's courage that counts."

I was a scared little kid. Sometimes for good reason. On one occasion, my father had me with him when he visited an office building in Jersey City, a strange place for me. He parked me on

---

* From Act III, *Lady Windermere's Fan* (1893).

the stairs between floors and said, "Wait here, I'll be back soon." I was about eight, and this alone could result in arrest for child abuse today.

Strangers passed me left and right; no one stopped or even cast a smile, and I thought hours had elapsed. Finally, he retrieved me. (I found out later he was visiting still another usurious lending operation to try to pay off other debts.)

Sometimes there was no good reason for my fears. I felt that any changes in routine were threatening, strangers were threatening, the omnipresent monsters under my bed were threatening—and when I saw the original *War of the Worlds* I couldn't sleep for a week.

I had no courage.

In school, I was driven by an urge not to fail, with all of its stigma and ramifications. I wanted the best picture, the best sandbox distribution, the best voice, the best test results. What quickly emerged, however, was that this was the express lane to failure because I could not excel in those areas—I'm a lousy artist, have a terrible singing voice, and someone always studied harder than I did.

But then I started learning from the failures instead of running from them. We can treat failure as cathartic, or it can weigh us down like the mob burying our feet in cement.

Mindsets: If you're not failing, you're not trying.

In the course of my life I have failed at:

- Getting into an Ivy League school
- Getting past a week of law school*

---

* I admit some of you might not consider that a failure. It was night school, during my days at Prudential. I was seeking a student deferment.

- Avoiding at least six auto accidents
- Staying out of serious debt (twice)
- Staying employed as a CEO for more than eighteen months
- Learning to play the piano, even in a rudimentary way
- Learning to swim very well
- Sailing
- Cooking anything (I can barely make a sandwich)
- Going past Life Scout in the Boy Scouts
- Closing a deal for a reality show on consulting
- Being able to control my impatience levels
- Making it past the first round on *Jeopardy*
- Recognizing that the woman in the elevator with me was Michelle Pfeiffer

And these are just my most memorable failures. For those who claim they have never failed, whether at closing a deal or mastering a new skill, I'd caution that one of three conditions obtain:

1. They have never undertaken anything really serious.
2. They have failed but don't realize it.
3. They are lying.

Students at military academies study great defeats, not just victories. They want to ensure they don't replicate past mistakes. I've never had a hard time with someone doing something wrong, such as not validating that the person in front of them is actually a potential customer or client. But I have a very tough time with anyone who *repeatedly* fails to validate that condition.

We learn from failures if we're smart.

Thus, we need to promote and exploit such learning. We need to ask the buyer *who rejected our proposal*: "What could I have done differently to have earned your trust and obtained this project?" We need to find out from family members what we did less than well when there's a blowup and a breakdown in communication. It's not so bad that it occurred, but it's horrid to allow one's ignorance of cause to allow the blowup to reoccur.

When you walk into a prospect's office or a job interview or a meeting where you need to garner support, remember this: *You cannot walk out poorer than when you entered.* You may not have the business or the position or the backing, but you will have learned something, in any case. If it's impossible to emerge poorer than when you entered, what on earth can stop you from entering? This isn't the Coliseum, where only one fighter will live.

The Wright brothers, Thomas Edison, Barbra Streisand, Guglielmo Marconi, Henry Ford, Steve Jobs, Michelangelo, Alexander Graham Bell, Jonas Salk, Abraham Lincoln, Ulysses S. Grant, Jack Welch, Meryl Streep, Frank Sinatra, Margaret Thatcher, Christopher Columbus: they all failed before, during, and/or after they succeeded. They learned from trial and error.

I've found that the key to startling success is to be fearless.* I don't mean reckless or foolhardy, and I don't mean imprudent. I mean fearless, because there is nothing to fear in our professions and businesses, assuming you're not a chain saw juggler (I actually know two) or a high-wire performer (I know one of those, also). Even when you're involved in tough and brutal professions, fearing failure will undermine you immediately. Prizefighters can't get in the ring afraid. My favorite Mike Tyson quote: "Everyone who gets in the ring has a plan until they are punched in the jaw."†

---

* Chapter 10 addresses "no fear."
† Quoted in *Sun Sentinel*, November 9, 2012, http://articles.sun-sentinel.com /2012-11-09/sports/sfl-mike-tyson-explains-one-of-his-most-famous-quotes -20121109_1_mike-tyson-undisputed-truth-famous-quotes.

Failure is only fatal when we allow it to be. When we curl up in the fetal position, or become depressed, or seek only to commiserate with others in the same boat, *then* failure can be fatal, at least metaphorically.

The greatest manifestation of perceived failure that we encounter these days is self-imposed victimization. Once we surrender accountability for our actions and fate and assign it to other forces, we become professional victims. (Definition: "Professional: Engaged in an activity as one's main occupation." This is starting to bug me.) Victimization is fatal, because we surrender control and merely complain. We no longer work to succeed; we spend our time and energy *trying to identify and validate to others why it's impossible for us to succeed.*

When we fail to find the *cause* of our failure in any activity, and instead assign it to the fates or the world or the winds, then we are reaching a fatal condition. I use "fatal" in the sense of ending our professional or business lives. Once we're convinced we can't help ourselves, but must rely on someone or some group that may not even realize we blame them for our condition, we are psychologically enslaved.

The inside track to success is more like a steeplechase than a marathon. We negotiate hurdles, wind, water hazards, and other runners. *But once around that course, and it should be familiar to us.* If we keep slipping in the same place or making the same inadequate leap, then it's no longer the course, it's us. We haven't learned from our previous falls. The course isn't conspiring against us; we're inadequate in our learning from the experience.

One of the fundamental issues in both fear and failure is the condition of our egos. Ironically, ego is that part of us that can't be physically bruised, but so often seems to take a beating.

Resilience and Ego

The ego represents a person's sense of importance and self-worth. In psychoanalysis, it is that aspect of your thinking that tests reality and provides a sense of personal identity.

That identity is carefully protected. We will go to great lengths to preserve what we consider to be our identity, and we make great effort to fight off perceived threats to it.

Unfortunately, we make way more of this than we should.

We fear our ego being damaged—our sense of self-worth—and we actually engage in dysfunctional and harmful activities to protect it. For example:

- We don't take chances with our opinions. We self-edit and become mute rather than risk someone pointing out we're wrong or, worse, laughing at us.
- We don't make phone calls if we feel we may be rejected. We take rejection personally rather than as a normal occurrence in business.
- We don't innovate. We stay with the tried and true. We become the 450,000th person talking about team building rather than the first person pointing out that companies rarely have teams (they usually have committees).
- We withdraw. We may try to hit a golf ball or sing or make a speech in the solitude of our office or bedroom, but not in front of others, especially others we deem to be more qualified and talented than we are.
- We don't push back and oppose. We become herd animals rather than lone wolves.

When I worked with Prudential Insurance in Newark, New Jersey, I was entrusted with a state-of-the-art (at the time) project to depict the need for insurance, designed to be delivered in a dramatic setting, using a recording keyed to an automatic projector. I was given months, a production crew, and facilities.

It looked great when we completed it, and my boss invited key people from other offices to watch the "premiere." Of course, a technical glitch threw the timing off, so there was laughter on the speakers when the slides showed a funeral, and people in the room were grimacing in pain. We ended early, and my boss said he didn't know whether to kill me or disown me.

I let my wife know it might be the end of me at Prudential, but, strangely, the next day no one mentioned it. It was old news, water under one hundred bridges.

I was fine.

I've known quite a few people (not to mention me) who went broke but discovered that when there wasn't another cent there was another day. Once you understand that when the presumed "worst" occurs, and you're still here with friends and prospects for a better life (it can't get worse), your ego toughens up because you're no longer afraid of it being damaged.

This is the heart of resilience, the ability to bounce back into form, spring back into shape, return to former health. Resilience has speed as its main fuel. The faster you return to form, the better off you are.

Mindsets: You will win and you will lose. None of this has an impact on your worth as a person.

In high school, I faced the horrifying prospect of serving as the emcee at assemblies (this was the burden of being president of the student council). Some eight hundred kids sat in the seats, knowing they would hate the content of the presentation no matter what it was, and I had to settle them down and introduce the visiting lecturer, the police chief, the health official, the amateur play, and so forth.

One day, the highly popular captain of the cheerleading team was asking for support, and as she left the stage she impulsively kissed me on the cheek at the lectern. When I spoke my voice was two octaves higher, and the place roared.

I realized at that moment how to control the assemblies, and I used humor for the rest of my term. It worked spectacularly.

I use humor all the time today, mostly the self-effacing variety. People enjoy humor at your expense (rather than at their own), and it eases tension and creates a common bond. I was in a tense meeting one day, and the client's assigned pit bull kept asking me *how* I would do this and *how* I would do that, insisting on free consulting.

Finally, at a point when he asked, "And how do we know that this will begin at that point?" I responded, "Because at that point you hand me the check." The buyer roared, the tension was gone, and the project locked up.

If you want to make it as an entrepreneur, your mindset must be "egoless." That is, you have to check your ego at the door. You can't attempt to outgun, outwit, and outperform everyone else around. You simply have to convince your buyer (or the person you're trying to influence) that you have great value to contribute. Occasionally, that doesn't work out, and your resilience will help you to simply move on. (I picture this as a coat check in a fancy restaurant, where they take your ego at the door for safekeeping, and on the way out you tip the coat check person whether you've had a good meal or not, as a sign of resilience.)

No one pushes me around, but I don't try to avoid situations where that might happen. My ego isn't subject to being hurt by someone else. I don't beat myself up when things go wrong. And when things do go south, I move my resilience into seventh gear and make myself healthy again.

What do you need for rapid resilience? I'd suggest the following:

- Ignore unsolicited feedback. It's virtually always for the sender. Don't become a bouncing ball in a pachinko machine.
- Learn to say no without justification. We get "trapped" into situations that can be quite damaging. You can say no to a request to head a fundraising committee, perform a pro bono service, or invite someone you dislike to an event. You don't need a justification. You're not on trial.
- Learn something from every endeavor. When I've been rejected for a project, I always have asked, "Would you take a minute to educate me about what I could have done better to win your business?"
- Look out the windshield, not the rearview mirror. Focus on what's ahead, not the road already traveled. And keep moving. If you are going fifty miles an hour and then stop, all that dust you generated will catch up and envelop you.
- Treat yourself well after a "loss," not only after a "win." You're not rewarding failure in so doing, but rewarding a good attempt and the right behaviors. In large organizations, I've always recommended that they reward behaviors, not solely victories.

The stronger your ego, the better your resilience. The better your resilience, the stronger your ego. They are completely synergistic, and you determine their strength and speed.

If they are in good shape, you can better assess prudent risk and have confidence in your own judgment.

Evaluating Upside/Downside

I've learned that certain people and professions are invariably and ineluctably conservative. I've experienced too many general counsels who advise their CEO—my client—not to act because of the risks. Let's face it, if corporate lawyers had their way, the company would remain closed, with the lights off and the doors locked, because then *nothing* could happen to cause grief.

Well, except lost profits, furious customers, and public ridicule. But I guess those aren't as bad as a lawsuit from someone tripping on the escalators.

There was a risk in most endeavors I undertook. One risk was in trying to be first, because you might be wrong, look bad, or just seem obsequious.* There was, of course, also a risk in waiting, because you might miss out if there were nothing left.

Wait a minute—risk in action and risk in inaction? What kind of odds are those?

I developed an internal risk/reward system that I later codified and that appears below. It struck me that *every truly important decision* has a risk element. As Robert Heinlein posited in *The Moon Is a Harsh Mistress*, TINSTAAFL (there is no such thing as a free lunch). Being assertive with a prospect might mean demonstrating your enthusiasm, but there is a risk that you might seem too aggressive. Being more passive might indicate you're a good listener, but you could be mistaken for having no views of your own.

Figure 2.1 demonstrates how I took the extremes and worked "inward" to determine optimal risk/reward scenarios for clients. You can easily change the definitions to apply to personal actions:

+1: Barely noticed improvement
+2: Minor but helpful benefits
+3: Strong benefits, noticed by others

---

* This is why I lost badly in the first round of the TV game show *Jeopardy* to a dancing waiter from Iowa. I kept trying to buzz in early and was locked out for five seconds. I guess he had better rhythm.

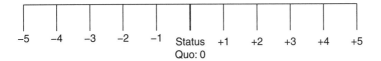

Question: What is the best and worst that might result?

+5= Paradigm-breaking improvement, industry leader
+4= Dramatic improvement, major publicity
+3= Strong benefits, organization-wide
+2= Minor benefits, localized
+1= Very minor improvement, barely noticed

−1= Very minor setback, barely noticed
−2= Minor setback, controlled locally
−3= Public setback, requires damage control
−4= Major defeat, financial damages, recovery time needed
−5= Devastating losses

Figure 2.1: Risk/Reward Balance

+4: Dramatic improvement, changes status and others' regard

+5: Life-altering improvement

-1: Minor inconvenience not requiring action

-2: Minor setback, requires correction at some point

-3: Obvious problem, requires fast and visible correction

-4: Public embarrassment, hard to recover

-5: Life- or health-threatening loss

In business, you can estimate what this means for your growth, profitability, and sustainability. Personally, you can judge what this means for your relationships and interactions. For example:

- Do you publicly declare that you're going to lose fifty pounds or run a marathon next year?

- Do you attempt to reconcile a tenuous relationship with a loved one?

- Do you take a loan to invest in the future success of your business?
※• Do you bring on employees to help in expansion?

The answer isn't yes or no, despite these being binary (yes or no) questions. The answer is that it depends on the risk-to-reward ratio. It's crazy to attempt an initiative or project that holds the potential for +5 reward *but also* -5 risk. A +3 to a -4 range seems far too risky. We'd all like a +5 to a -1, but life isn't like that. Generally, the more potential reward, the more potential risk. Just consider the stock market or Las Vegas (which many people consider one and the same).

The answer is that it depends *on what you can do to mitigate the risk.* You can try to prevent people from tripping on those escalators without closing down the building, and you can carry insurance in case the clumsy fools trip anyway (or cause a human pileup when they stop at the bottom to gaze around as if they've landed on a new planet). The problem with many corporate initiatives and personal plans is that we jump on the bandwagon of benefit without considering how to lessen risk.

Mindsets: Assertive risk management will safeguard your plans and enable you to be more daring and bolder than others.

Risk has two components:

1. Probability: This is the likelihood that an event will occur.
2. Seriousness: This is the impact of the event if it does occur.

Listen up: *Most people overestimate probability and underestimate seriousness.*

I used to dream up things that a prospect would say in a first meeting, such as:

Where did you go to school?
How much do you know about the widget business?
What happens if you die before the project is completed?
Do you have at least one hundred people in your operation?

None of these was ever asked.* About 99.8 percent of all prospects I've met have been pleasant people who wanted to investigate whether I had value and could help them.

However, we often miscalculate the seriousness of a bad first impression. We don't prepare well by learning the company's background, or we arrive like a pack animal with fifty pounds of equipment, or we're groomed poorly, or use passive language. We only get one first impression. If we blow it, *that's serious.*

We can reduce the probability of an event by finding the likely causes and eliminating them to the extent possible: if smoking causes fires, put up "no smoking" signs. If combustibles cause fire, set up separate areas, isolating them. If we might ruin something we're building around the house because we've not done it before, read the instructions before beginning or find someone with experience to help. If we want our kids to listen, perhaps we should set that example by listening first.

We can ameliorate the seriousness of an event by seeking to mitigate the effects. We can install a sprinkler system and buy insurance. We can have extra materials on hand in case we ruin the ones we're using.

Note that no matter how effective the reduction of the

---

* Well, I'm asked about what happens if I die. I respond that I'm Catholic and assume I'd go to heaven.

effects—contingent action—may be, the problem has occurred. Thus, we can't afford to underestimate seriousness. The key is prevention, but that requires a focus on *probable causes* and not just any cause. The client isn't likely to say, "Did you get an MBA from Harvard?" but is likely to say, "What do you think you can do for me?" Which is the question you should prepare for?

Thus, seek to maintain the reward side of the ratio but reduce the risk side. That balance might differ for each of us, depending on our boldness and confidence. But we're talking about finding "net" risk, that is, risk *after* we institute means to prevent it and/or deal with it.

But our risk taking shouldn't vary based on foolhardiness.

CHAPTER 3

Gaining Influence

Too many people ease up around the turns in life. Life isn't a marathon but a constant series of sprints. Speed is as important as content— I know that's heresy—but we live in a world of instant gratification, where instant response usually carries the day.

Once upon a time, I would walk into a room of colleagues and begin metaphorically shooting—using volume, argument, sarcasm, and biased examples. Once they were all "dead," I'd say, "Fine, then you do see it my way, right?"

I won a lot of shootouts, but not commitment and not many friends.

Treat Others As They Expect to Be Treated

The Golden Rule about treating others the way you'd like to be treated has stood the test of time in many environments and circumstances. But I found it's not entirely accurate.

A lot of people don't want to be treated the way you would like to be treated yourself. And it's very difficult for many of us to understand how others would like to be treated unless we abandon the bromide and forget about ourselves for the moment.

I worked my way through college, partially at the main post office in Union City, New Jersey. In those days of "yore," as my son is fond of saying,* nearly everything was done by hand, from sorting the mail to cancelling the stamps. The restroom stalls had no doors, so that postal inspectors behind one-way mirrors could ensure there was no theft being carried out. Some of the assignments were horrid (painting mailboxes in 110-degree heat), and some truly frightening (when I finished a complete route in a truck by 11:30 a.m., six mailmen cornered me and told me if I ever returned again before the 5:00 p.m. quitting time they'd break my legs). I had to join the union and I had to watch my step.

A guy named Burt Herring was the supervisor who handed out assignments to part-timers and could even change the routes of the regular employees. I noticed that everyone immediately called him "Burt," even on first introduction, but I also noticed that he wore a shirt and tie every day and clearly considered himself a respectable manager.

So, I immediately began addressing him as "Mr. Herring."

A lot of my colleagues made fun of me, but I began to get choice assignments, the coveted overtime hours (so lucrative I funded my girlfriend's—yes, she's now my wife—engagement ring), and no harassment from anyone within Burt's sight or hearing.

I had not realized it, but I was treating the man the way he thought he should be treated, with the respect I could provide, which was a simple "Mr." I despise the practice today of every teller, serviceperson, contractor, and dog walker calling me "Alan." Why not at least start with an honorific, and see if I invite you to call

---

* "You were *alive* when Kennedy was shot?!" he exclaimed at dinner one night as my wife and I recalled the Dallas disaster. "Yes," I said, "but you should have been with me at Ford's Theatre!"

me "Alan"? We've had a wonderful young couple housesitting for us and watching our dogs for ten years. We attended their wedding. I invited them to call me "Alan."

"Oh, no," they said, "we wouldn't be comfortable."

Are you treating others the way *they would like to be treated*? Have you even bothered to find out what that would look like? It may well be different from the way you would like to be treated (you might prefer that people use your first name and become immediately friendly).

When I meet someone I want to influence—a buyer, a board member, someone in government, an investor—I wait to see how they want to be addressed. I'll say, "Ms. Johnson, nice to finally meet you," and if she says, "Please call me Marilyn," I'll do so. If she doesn't, I will not. When someone writes me a letter starting with "Dear Mr. Weiss," I write back using the proper honorific. (In Germany, this becomes fascinating, because they accrete honorifics the way the Spanish do family names, so you can wind up with "Herr Dr. Professor Smit.")

I find that people generally like to be treated consistently with their perceptions of their:

- Position in business
- Position socially (e.g., donor, patron of the arts)
- Accomplishments
- Education
- Family status*
- Culture and origins
- Values and beliefs
- Abilities and disabilities

---

* Vitally important, given same-sex marriage, life partners instead of spouses, and so forth.

I was at a huge conference, and a particularly well-known and accomplished member of the association was present, restricted to a wheelchair because of advancing muscular dystrophy. I watched as everyone stood around, trying to include her in the conversation as though there were nothing irregular about the dynamic.

I went over and knelt next to her wheelchair. We had an animated conversation, until I was called away. She said to me as I left, "Alan, I can't thank you enough for being polite and considerate and coming down to my level." Others thought she wanted to be treated as if she were the same as they were. I realized she wanted to be treated in a manner consistent with her disability and needed some accommodation.

People are quite different, from you and from one another. The secret of our success is to understand to the best of our ability how others would prefer that we treat them, not to treat them as we think we'd want to be treated (and in the case of the wheelchair, I have no idea how I'd like to be treated because I had never had to consider it).

We all have native behaviors that serve as a sort of "home base" because we're so comfortable there. We may change, of course, depending on the environment, the issue, and the other performers. But left to our own devices, we tend to stay "at home." The key is the flexibility to change as needed, to treat people as they wish to be treated. I'm very impatient and action oriented, and I hate to waste time on small talk, but I realize that many people whom I want to influence or merely make happy require social interaction and time to digest conversations. *Hence, it's incumbent upon me to make that alteration in my own behavior if I want to influence their behavior.*

Mindsets: The only "type" of personality style you should aim for is "flexible"!

This is precisely why I despise "personality tests" and behavioral predictions and labels. (What do you expect from a "High D, impulsive/compressive, green, G3, inattentive"?) They induce us to explain away behavior rather than understand it, to seek certain "desirable" typing rather than learn to adapt.

The most successful personality types I know of are "flexible"! You'll go much further faster trying to treat people the way they prefer to be treated. Speaking of further faster...

Getting There Firstest with the Mostest

"Getting there firstest with the mostest" was the response of Confederate general Nathan Bedford Forrest, a notorious cavalry irregular and raider, when asked how he won so many battles against better organized troops.*

About seventy-five years later, Damon Runyon, the Broadway reporter, wit, and man-about-town, famously observed: "The battle isn't always to the strong nor the race to the swift, but that's the way to bet."

I found that when I showed up early for a Little League game I was often inserted into the starting lineup, even though there were kids with more talent at the position. But the coach didn't want to worry about whether they'd show up or not and perhaps play havoc with his plans. I actually made the all-star team my final year, pretty much based on Woody Allen's tenet that "80 percent of success is just showing up." I'd amend that to read: "and the other 20 percent is in showing up *early*."

---

* There is some debate about this, since some historians feel he was an educated person who used proper grammar, but the quote remains with us and is instructive.

I always arrived at buyers' offices thirty minutes early. I'd bring a book or read the client's annual report, but I wanted to make sure that I was never late, thereby missing an appointment with a busy executive. Half the time I was invited in early and gained extra, precious time to influence my prospect.

I'm always early at airports, trains, and boats. Sometimes I can catch an earlier one, sometimes I'll relax in their club, sometimes I schmooze with the staff and can make special requests.

At a workshop I ran in Boston, one woman walked in five minutes late and had to take the only remaining seat, which was still empty because it wasn't a very good one. Later, she actually complained about it. "I can help you," I said. "Tomorrow, come earlier."

In business and often in life, *speed is as important as content.* That is, success always trumps perfection. Perfection is the archenemy of excellence, because the insistence on (the impossible) perfection eternally stalls any meaningful action. Every plane you take, dinner you eat, car you drive, medical office you visit, and friend you trust is imperfect. If we insisted on consistent perfection we would barely be able to feed ourselves, much less conduct business.

When a client contact tells me on site, "The larger project has to be approved by my boss" or "There's someone here in charge of Europe who could use similar help," I always respond, "Can we stop by and meet while I'm here?" I never wanted to delay the introduction or contact. Many of them said, "I'm free for lunch, can you hang around for an hour?"

Disney is famous for providing the *perception* of speed. The long lines continually move because they are so long, and signs proclaim, "You're now only thirty minutes from the thrill of this ride!" Contrast that with most TSA operations in U.S. airports, which seem as though people have put down roots. (British Airways, terminal five, in Heathrow has an ingenious way to create speed in very thorough security checkpoints. It can be done.)

In this age of immediate gratification, people don't like waiting, and certainly not for "perfection." They'd rather obtain something good immediately. I return all of my calls within ninety minutes during business hours, and all of my e-mail within two hours. This isn't a matter of hard work, just disciplined responsiveness, and with current technology it's easier than ever.

Speed is infectious. You create a greater sense of urgency on the part of others when they see it in you.

Heft is the other part of Forrest's point ("mostest").

We need to have substance. We need to have valuable insights, commentary, and advice. So many people are afraid that others will steal their ideas and intellectual property that they hide them under the mattress to protect them. And they gain just as much interest as money gains under a mattress.

Have you watched the disguised infomercials, where a former politician or coach or businessperson is almost literally propped up to "interview" someone? That someone has paid at least $15,000— and sometimes five times that—for the phony interview with a has-been that everyone knows was paid for. Just yesterday I was offered the "opportunity" to appear in a documentary about coaches—for a $90,000 investment!

Getting there with heft means having metaphors, examples, and illustrations of what the prospect or other party can profit from, in return for which you receive serious consideration for your proposal, idea, or request. You are reading my sixtieth book right now, which shows just how unconcerned I am about placing my IP in the public forum. If simply reading a book were sufficient, the books would cost $250,000 each and there would be no consultants. But that's not, and never will be, the case.

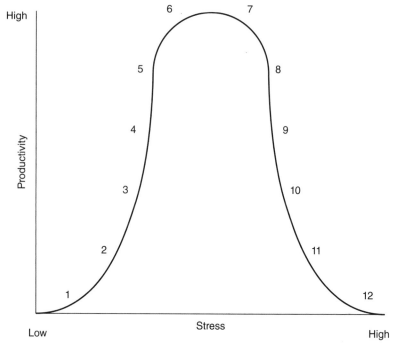

Figure 3.1: The Stress Bell Curve

Visual heft is illustrated by the graphic you see in figure 3.1. It makes the simple case that too little stress results in low productivity (bottom left) because no one has the urgency to act, but too much stress (bottom right) *also* results in low productivity because people are scared to death. The idea is not to drive them from the extreme left to the extreme right, but rather to the middle, position 6–7, where just enough stress creates urgency and the adrenaline rush required for high performance. Eliminating stress isn't only impossible, but wrong.*

That one graph and single paragraph should be very convincing, and should foster a discussion about how to accomplish that appropriate

---

* See my book, with Richard Citrin, *The Resilience Advantage* (New York: Business Expert Press, 2016).

stress level, personally and organizationally. That's quick and that's heft, yet it also promotes the behavior that you need to get to know me better because you're wondering: What other value do I have in store for you? (You'll find it throughout this book, but you'll find more if you hire me!) Speed and heft are hard to beat. They may not always triumph, but that is "the way to bet." Perfection is the enemy of speed and heft, but resistance is not! Objections are a sign of interest, tough questions a sign of curiosity. What you don't want is apathy, which is anathema to achieving your goals with others.

So, don't be afraid of provocation and the ensuing debate, no matter how rough. Getting there quickly and early will provide more time for debate, and having a great value to display will keep others mesmerized while you head for your destination.

How to Compromise and Do It Your Way

When I was in grade school the place to go was Palisades Amusement Park, an iconic institution on the cliffs above the Hudson River across from New York, just north of Manhattan. In those days the park had rides, exhibits, features, a saltwater pool (with waves), and the latest doo-wop groups singing on an outdoor stage.* Alas, today the area is the home of a colossal, dreary set of high-rise apartment buildings.

One of the rides back then consisted of small boats that seated four people, with one behind the steering wheel. The boats had no propulsion or real steering; the flow in the channel carried them around a series of turns and straightaways until they were back at the start. If the boat wandered too far left or right, it merely bounced off the sides of the channel and continued to be guided by the thrust of the current.

---

* The Palisades are a topographic "intrusive sill." Read the epilogue to find out how I know this and why it's important.

We need to use the same principle in guiding our conversations today. The destination is what we decide it is, usually agreement on a project, a position, or a site for a vacation. If we keep that destination firmly fixed in our mind and create the correct current, we can set up the "walls" that keep the boat in the channel always heading for the end of our ride.

No wind is a good wind if we don't know our destination.

Too many of us allow conversations to drift, and even to radically shift, creating a floodplain instead of a ride in a specific stream. We allow others to ramble, or we digress ourselves, or we take "safe" courses of action, not wanting confrontation.

Here is how to keep conversation headed toward your destination if the other person keeps trying to strike out in other directions: interrupt. That's right, stop the person, even if it's a buyer. But do it with language like this:

- Excuse me, this is fascinating and I want to make sure I've captured that last point. In the context of this decision we're discussing, do you mean that you tend to accept more risk than most?
- May I stop you briefly? It seems that you've referred to unacceptable attrition—talent leaving—three times now. Is that correct?
- Pardon me for interrupting, but I'm not certain if you meant that sales should be better or margins should be better. Which is it?

In these examples, you have to be bold enough to barge in; taking the onus on yourself is necessary ("Sorry, my fault, but I think I missed the third point..."). You have to be able to relate the interruption to something—anything—the other party may have said and connect it with the route to your personal destination. You can accomplish this by staying in the moment during the diatribe—don't lull off. Listen for the "pivot point" where you can turn things around.

The key technique, which you see in the three examples above, is what I coined long ago as "rhetorical permission." With this technique, you ask to do something that can't be denied. You've experienced rhetorical greetings, such as "How are you?," where the other party really doesn't care, is merely opening dialogue, and if you were to respond, "Well, my knee hurts and I have some arthritis in my index finger, and the hives haven't fully disappeared…" you'd drive people from the room.

Thus, by asking, "May I…" or, "If you don't mind…" you'll create the new dynamic—changing the course of the conversation—in a polite, never denied, and firm manner.

> **Mindsets:** The art of the compromise is to protect your "musts" and negotiate away some "wants."

Here's how to keep conversations within the boat channel when you may tend to drift:

PAY ATTENTION!

That's it. Stay in the moment and be present, rather than planning your next sentence or furiously writing irrelevant notes or hoping to be liked, as if the conversation is a test and there are right answers. The only "answer" is the destination you have in mind. Focus on it, and don't ask irrelevant questions:

"Trying to get people to donate is as difficult as hitting a one iron."

WRONG: "You play golf? Have you ever played at the Coyote Club?"

RIGHT: "Well, here's my idea of how to put a putter in their hands and make it easy."

Finally, recognize your "musts." These are objectives or results or goals that are absolutely mandatory to your success, are clearly identifiable, and are reasonable. When we moved to California and were looking at homes outside San Francisco, I told the realtor that I must have air conditioning because I have pollen allergies. She showed us home after home that lacked it, but would say, "But you're only five minutes from the school," or "But this view is amazing," or "You're on the water!"

She wanted me to give up a must, and many people do, only to be miserable not long after. People often purchase cars, computers, vacation homes, investment vehicles, and so on that are in conflict with their musts, because they don't separate them from their wants.

If you want to compromise and still get results in your favor:

- Demonstrate value for the other people involved.
- Protect your personal "musts."
- Don't allow the other person to drift out of the channel.
- Don't drift out of the channel yourself.

The Power of the Calming Voice

Enthusiasm is great, except when it's transmogrified into blind zeal. People with passion seek to influence, but zealots seek to convert. Those seeking converts cannot compromise. You can't proselytize to a partial position. (Okay, you have something of a point; I'll believe in God on Mondays, Wednesdays, and Fridays.)

Gaining influence is not about taking prisoners. It's not about changing behaviors 180 degrees.

Mindsets: Consensus is something you can live with, not something you'd die for.

Once upon a time I embraced "firstest with the mostest" in *all* situations, regardless of context and irrespective of whether I already had the business. I wanted to solve the problem first, be first with the "right" answer, show that I was on top of things.

But personal and organizational issues are not always simple, and even when they are, *you can't get away with a simple suggestion because the perception is that you haven't spent enough time considering it.* Therefore, we need analyses, assessments, advance work, preparatory work, pilots, and failure work. We not only have to develop an effective solution or recommendation, but we have to make it appear as if it were the result of careful contemplation and not a knee-jerk response.

Yet one of the reasons I left corporate organizational development work was that I knew there were—literally—eleven causes solely or in combination responsible for 98 percent of all issues, yet I had to arrive at my conclusions through circuitous routes.* I could tell a client, "If it hurts when you do that, stop doing it," but that advice would be accepted after five days, not five minutes.

So I developed another technique, which I've always referred to as "the calming voice." This is an intervention whereby I listen (apparently carefully, but often tediously) to the various inputs and contributions to a decision or problem or plan. I let others wear themselves out and exhaust all possible inputs. I wait for a brief silence, and then I say, "Perhaps I could summarize where I think we are and what we should do." The others welcome hearing from a

---

* See the appendix if you'd like to know what they are, with my compliments.

new voice in the current discussion, hoping I'll lend heft to their side of the debate.

It's important, when employing the calming voice, to use a visual aid. It needn't be fancy and should never look as if it was prepared in advance, else all the spontaneity so important for influence here evanesces. A flip chart, whiteboard, or chalkboard is best, so that everyone can focus on what you depict at the same time.

Here's one example:

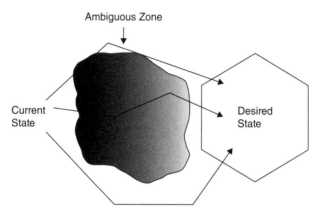

Figure 3.2: Visual Example of Calming Voice Process

I call the graphic in figure 3.2 a "process visual," because it denotes a process visually.* In this case, it shows the state where people currently are, and my calming voice description of the future state:

> On the right is what I'm hearing is the future state that all of you aspire to. I think the differences expressed are in how to get there. That's because it's never been done, and we have an

---

* See my books *The Great Big Book of Process Visuals* (East Greenwich, RI: Las Brisas Research Press, 2009) and *Son of Process Visuals* (East Greenwich, RI: Las Brisas Research Press, 2011).

"ambiguous zone" in the middle. We have to decide whether to go around it or through it, but in either case we need to show people the way. Would you all agree with this?

I'd now focus on the ambiguous zone and how to handle it—not by assuring people of the route, because we don't know what's in there, but by assuring them we will lead the way with what light we have. Suddenly, we have agreement.

I've used this technique when I spoke at school board meetings, when I chaired the town's planning board, when I chaired the Newport International Film Festival, and when I worked with JPMorgan Chase, Toyota, Mercedes, Bank of America, the American Institute of Architects, and scores of other organizations public and private, large and small, for profit and nonprofit.

The key is to appear as if you've carefully considered all others' inputs to that point (even if the answer was as obvious to you as a ham sandwich, not uncommon with a good intellect) and have applied some ratiocination; then, hold back until argument is at least temporarily exhausted.

All sides will be thirsty for a voice of reason at that point, especially one that doesn't declare a "winner" so much as an exit. All that's required is some creative thinking.

CHAPTER 4

Critical Thinking Skills

Consciousness is a factor of how fast we process information. A dog has a higher consciousness than a rabbit, but many people have higher consciousness levels than other people. Information processing is a learnable skill, based on asking the right questions to generate the right answers. Most people are asking the wrong questions.

How to Create Your Own System of Success

My therapist said to me once, "Alan, you have your own set of pipes, intricately constructed, which only you can play." Little did I know how hugely insightful that was (and for only $120 for fifty-five minutes).

A fascinating—and retrograde—aspect of human performance is that we tend to start similar projects and activities as if we've never performed them before. We insist on reinventing the wheel and never improve upon it. We don't trust ourselves to rely on our past success—or even past failures. We're supposed to learn from success and failures to make us more effective in the future.

Yet it's as if we are still using solid rubber tires and complaining about the bumps.

We often wind up in a real-world Monopoly game, continually drawing the card that says, "Go directly to jail, do not pass GO, do not collect $200." Welcome to *Groundhog Day*.*

There are universal systems of success. For example, we know that there is a relationship between cause and effect, or action and reaction (and I'll cover this later in this chapter). We know that debits and credits should even out in accounting, and that we can't expect results without accountability. Yet we also maintain that the definition of insanity is doing the same thing over and over and expecting different results.

Are we all mad?

Think back to a recent instance where you helped someone. It could be formally—professionally, for a fee—or informally—personally, as a friendly gesture. Write here the problem or issue that constituted the reason for your involvement:

_____

Now write here the primary action you took to improve the situation:

_____

Finally, explain here the improved condition that resulted:

_____

What you've just explained is:

- Situation
- Intervention
- Resolution

_____

* For those of you who eschew modern entertainment, this was the movie in which the protagonist is forced to keep living the exact same day over and over.

Congratulations, you have a coaching protocol. You've just codified, in sixty seconds or less, a coaching system that you needn't re-create in the future. You have a model, a process, *a methodology,* even if you're not a professional coach.

How do you make decisions? You probably determine what you want to accomplish (choose a vacation destination, make a new hire), examine alternatives (beach/mountains/cruise, job candidates), and look at any risks (bad weather/crowds, lack of experience). Then you make a balanced decision, weighing benefits and risks. Thus:

- Objectives
- Alternatives
- Risk

And there's your decision-making methodology!

These are your "systems of success." You have to move from unconscious competency to conscious competency to understand your own processes and enable yourself to replicate them and repeat them. (Your personal "pipes.") You may have systems for success in the way you run meetings, deal with your kids, overcome unexpected adversity, sell new business, or establish budgets. Those times when you're less successful than others *are probably instances in which you've departed from your success system unwittingly because you haven't sufficiently incorporated it into your unconscious competency.*

Mindsets: We learn in "conscious competency" and incorporate success on a regular basis by making such learning "unconscious competency."

I've found that a smile and early humor create the right frame of mind with large audiences in a speech or with a small group in a conference room. Once I realized that, it became an automatic response to such environments. When I was unsuccessful at times getting the audience to warm up to me, I realized later that I had departed from my normally unconscious competency, because I was distracted or worried about some unrelated issue.

Therapists, doctors, CPAs, attorneys, coaches, salespeople—and high performers in general—all follow a highly uniform set of protocols in meeting new patients/clients/customers, reacting to what they learn, reaching conclusions, validating assumptions, and so forth. While this isn't as apparent in some fields, such as art or design, if you examine the procedures used you'll find that there are constants, such as lighting, proportion, and flow.

I've met thousands of excellent executives in my career. About half would tell me that they operate by "gut feel" or being "in the moment." But that's not the case at all. Almost every one of them, once I probed, had a *system* or *procedure* they utilized, which they either couldn't or wouldn't articulate at the time. But with observation and questioning, the processes always emerged. People don't achieve excellence by trial and error. They achieve it by being right, by winning, by succeeding *most of the time*. That level of success is neither accidental nor dependent on reinventing an approach each time.

My first accountant told me that he could look just at cash at the beginning of a time period and cash at the end, and figure out everything else he had to know. I can look at three points in a consultant's proposal for a project and immediately assess its value and probability of success.

Imagine the time that's saved when compared with those who might achieve the same results but only after laborious reading and repetitive actions?

I've always believed in Tools for Change: The 1% Solution®. Simply stated: improve by 1 percent a day and in seventy days you're twice as good. (It's the miracle of compound interest; try it on a calculator.) For some of you, the 1 percent for today may just be this: you already possess highly successful processes that have accounted for your success. But you may not have codified them and incorporated them sufficiently in unconscious competency to be achieving full value from them.

Think about not only *when* you succeed, but *why* you succeed. The "why" will force you to examine the processes you used to accomplish the goals. Don't settle for others saying, "Good job!" Ask them why they think so.

Those are the routes and tools to create your "personal pipes."

Finding Cause, Not Blame

In most work and social environments, the default position for tackling problems is to find blame. I know how cynical that sounds, but I also don't believe the government will operate within its revenues next year, and that's a sure bet, albeit highly cynical.

There is malicious blame pursuit: "You just can't rely on those salespeople, they lie when they say 'hello'"; "What do you expect from a boss whose only connection to the business is DNA?"

There is inadvertent blame pursuit: "We have to find the person in the warehouse who is no doubt to blame for all these delayed orders"; "The problem is that the R&D head has been traveling for most of the past month."

Nonetheless, we usually find someone to blame, rather than pursuing the most important thing: finding *cause*. (The cause could be an individual who is poorly trained or a saboteur, but that will emerge as we first search for cause.) We seldom say:

- Let's determine when and where the error occurred.
- Let's find out why this happened.
- Let's examine the facts first, not make baseless accusations.

Ah, but accusation provides for such immediate gratification, and immediately solves the problem! Or does it?

Perhaps *the* primary critical thinking skill is to organize around the fact that problems have causes and that the cause must be removed in order to remove the problem.

You can see in figure 4.1 that a problem—and the ensuing search for cause and not blame—consists of a three-part definition.*

1. There is a deviation of actual performance (or equipment, processes, or people) from the expected standard that had been the norm.
2. The cause is *unknown*. If you know the cause, then you are faced with a decision on to how to deal with it, not a problem to solve.
3. You care. If you don't care, you don't have a problem.

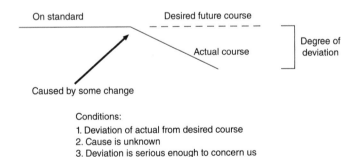

Conditions:
1. Deviation of actual from desired course
2. Cause is unknown
3. Deviation is serious enough to concern us

Figure 4.1: Problem-Solving Definition

---

* My source for this is Charles H. Kepner and Benjamin B. Tregoe, *The Rational Manager* (New York: McGraw-Hill, 1965). I was with their firm for eleven years, a combination of a boutique McKinsey and *Mad Men*.

Nowhere here do you see "blame" or "culpability" or "fault." The immediate reversion to finding *someone* to blame is an unfortunate human condition, and one you have to sacrifice if you're going to be an adept problem solver. And the reason for this topic is precisely because a Million Dollar Maverick is a superb and rapid problem solver.

So, while others waste time and energy shouting at each other and arguing about who is to blame, those of us on the fast track find out the cause of the problem—if it really is a problem—and move to take action. There are two kinds of actions available to you.

1. *Corrective action* removes the problem by removing the cause. If the roof is leaking and creating the problem (that is, the adverse effect) of wet floors and furniture, you repair the roof, either temporarily with a tarp or permanently with new asphalt, rubber, or shingles.

2. *Adaptive action* mitigates the effect while leaving the problem in place. Positioning a bucket under the leak will protect the furniture for now, until the roof is fixed.

Many years ago we owned an otherwise wonderful Jaguar sedan that was notorious for leaking oil. Repairs to the engine were expensive, took forever, and were not guaranteed to last. The adaptive action of putting a quart of oil in monthly was cheaper, faster, and removed any chance of adverse effects (engine burnout). That's how we adapted.

It did no good to blame Jaguar engineers or dealers or designers or mechanics, because we still would have had to deal with the problem. Which, in fact, we could do very easily.

When you blame others, you become enslaved to them. And they can't free you, because they are wholly unaware that they have become your captor! I've seen internecine battles within major clients, where silos of people spent most of their day blaming one another: home office versus field; sales versus R&D; accounting versus everyone; labor versus management; subordinates versus superiors. (This is why political polarization is so awful today—instead of correcting problems we blame the other side for them.)

Unfortunately, the same dynamic obtains in our lives. We blame our kids instinctively (who else would have left the refrigerator door open?). We blame our spouse or significant other (it's not the first time; you've done this before). We blame our neighbors (they must have had people over who dumped their garbage on our lawn). We even blame the dog (there's only one reason these new plants are dying).

Admit it—we tend to look for blame before cause, or we equate searching for cause with assigning blame!

> **Mindsets:** We need to stop blaming people so much, including ourselves.

There is one more important element on my simple chart. *All* problems are caused by some change. After all, if nothing changed, there would be no deviation from the normal, expected performance. But not all changes are equal. We should search solely for *relevant changes.*

How do we know what's relevant?

If you look at the arrow on the chart, it points to the position where the deviation first occurred. Ergo, *nothing after that point in time could have caused the problem, because the problem was already being experienced prior to such a change.* Hence, the "relevant changes" are those that occurred *prior to* the deviation.

If there was garbage on the lawn before the neighbor's party, then it couldn't have been distributed by the neighbor's guests. If the plants were dying before the dog was retrieved from the kennel, then it wasn't the poor dog. If sales declined prior to a new manager being assigned, then the sales decline could not have been caused by the new manager.

I think you can see that this reasoning is more than just somewhat useful. It's essential to rapid and accurate problem solving, because it thrusts the pursuit in the direction of solely relevant changes. (And in almost all cases, the change that was the cause of the problem is rather close to the departure of actual from expectation, as you might expect.)

If we combine the important pursuit of solving problems with these four principles, we will be at the Sherlock Holmes level of noticing that the dog did not bark in the night:

1. A true problem has three composite elements.
2. We cannot default to the simplistic notion of finding someone to blame as a starting point.
3. To remove a problem the cause of the problem has to be removed, and the cause is always a relevant change.
4. We can opt to remove the cause once we know it, or choose to mitigate (or merely live with) the effects.

Welcome to the ranks of the finest maverick problem solvers.

Identifying Distinctions

One of the quickest problem-solving techniques I've devised is to rapidly look for distinctions. A distinction is a contrast *between similar things*.

If I ask you, "What's distinctive about a duck?," in most cases you'd answer:

- It quacks.
- It has webbed feet.
- It's semiaquatic and flies.
- It has feathers.
- It lays eggs.

As you can see, geese and gulls and other birds share these traits, and some people can quack just like a duck, and some birds can mimic the sound as well. These aren't really distinctions, because *there is no point of similar comparison.*

So the proper response to my question is this: *As compared to what?* As compared to geese, they are smaller and do not form life-long mating bonds. As compared to gulls, they are not protected, don't usually thrive in saltwater, and have more diversity.

Mindsets: The *tighter* the comparison, the more valid and useful the distinctions that result.

When I began coaching people, in the early days of my consulting practice, I noticed (perhaps "research" is too grand a concept in my profession), or more properly had thrust upon me, the fact that high-performing executives and low-performing executives had consistent traits—distinctions—in each category. So did salespeople, call center operators, restaurant servers, and contractors. (I began to apply this practice of making distinctions to everything, because it helps in hiring and selection.)

This collection of common traits I assembled into *patterns,* which, if positive, required reinforcement and, if negative, required replacement.*

For example, top-performing servers:

- Greeted people with a smile, simply announced their name, and immediately asked about beverages
- Provided the list of specials from memory, with enthusiasm and emphasis on personal favorites
- Alerted diners to any inadvertent delays in preparation
- Refilled soft drink glasses and asked about another alcoholic beverage
- Inquired whether guests were satisfied with the meal
- Offered desserts and after-dinner drinks with gusto: "Would you like one of our very low-calorie cheesecakes, or perhaps a glass of port?"

If you're curious about the outcomes of these behaviors, not only are gratuities higher, but sales of desserts and after-dinner drinks rise from 5 percent of diners to 25 percent of diners, and those two items are the highest-margin offerings on any menu.

Among the worst patterns of senior executives:

- Cutting off subordinates when they are talking
- Making rash decisions without validation
- Believing money is a primary motivator[†]
- Relying on credentials and education instead of behavior when hiring or making selection decisions
- Being oblivious to their role as exemplars

---

* I didn't know it at the time, but I was an early adherent of positive psychology, and realized that you can't "change" negative patterns of behavior; you have to replace them with positive ones that generate the same or a better reward.

† Primary motivators are actually gratification in one's work and autonomy.

Tracking these distinctive traits enables us to determine key issues, challenges, and obstacles rapidly, and to make our own decisions more clearly and rapidly. For example, I won't hire a contractor who takes more than twenty-four hours to return my calls. I won't hire a subcontractor for my business whose early questions are about expense reimbursement instead of the kinds of clients I deal with.

But here's the fundamental maverick lesson: organizations and people waste their time by looking for distinctions between *best and worst*. The key, useful, vital distinctions are between *best and next best*!

Organizations waste billions annually* on remedial training, trying to help the worst performers become average performers. That is not the way for organizations to thrive. The investment needs to be in the current all-stars and *those who can readily become all-stars*. Hence, by asking what's distinctive about your best performers as compared to the next best, you'll have tight distinctions. Note, for example:

- Their prior work history
- The first manager they were assigned to
- The mentoring they received
- The specific traits that set top performers apart

These are easily provided, once known. The gap (distinctions) between top performers and poor performers doesn't yield tight distinctions, and is often about attitude and energy. Enthusiasm can't be taught. These comparisons result in observations that poor performers:

---

* According to a variety of sources, including the Association for Talent Development, annual expenditures for training surpass $60 billion in the U.S. alone. Yes, that's ten zeros after the six.

- Show lack of initiative in asking for help
- Have an inability to apply what they see and hear
- Complain about work conditions
- Have excessive absences

If we examine our own lives, the question of why we're good at sailing but can't learn the piano may prompt a search for a good drink. But if we ask ourselves why we're good at sailing but not quite as good at giving directions or reading maps, we might come up with some solid distinctions that result in easy learning and improvement—that is, I took mandatory sailing lessons; perhaps I should take a course on map reading.

In business, look for distinctions that represent the kinds of people you want working for you, or whom you wish to be around if you're seeking a position (or being recruited). People who leave organizations don't leave the company, they leave their boss, in most cases. Money can't assuage a poor working relationship that one must face daily. What are the distinctive traits of the people you want around you?

When hiring for personal needs, ask yourself what kind of responsiveness, accountability, proaction, and work ethic you want to pay for. The cheaper labor may prove to be insufferable, far beyond the savings. If you're thinking of changing banks (or attorneys, CPAs, schools, and so forth), don't just waltz in to "get a feel for the place." Go in with a clear set of distinctions that would make the alternative stand out or fade into the herd. (When my kids changed schools, I asked the head of the middle school we were considering, "What's the biggest drawback here?" He looked at me, said he'd never been asked that, thought a moment, and then told me what they were. To me, that was the distinctive behavior I sought; everyone else was simply telling me they were perfect.)

What's distinctive about the absolute best experience you've had, compared with those that were good but not quite as impressive? That's the distinction that will truly tell you what's different about a duck.

If Nothing Changes, Nothing Happens

To this point, I've been discussing *reactions* to problems and challenges. But the true star performer is the one who *creates* new standards, who innovates. Here's one of those tight distinctions I talked about in the previous segment:

Opportunism: The ability to take advantage of positive or negative developments without having planned for them or expected them.

Innovation: The practice of creating new, pragmatic, useful ideas that don't solve past problems but instead establish new and higher standards.*

> **Mindsets:** Innovation is *applied* creativity. It is not merely the formulation of ideas (ideation) but the utilitarian application of them by others.

This is a world of volatile change. That is not about to alter. I am the eldest of the baby boomers, and I lived pretty much in a consistent cocoon through the 1950s. Black and white television became inconsistent color television, soldiers on the GI Bill came back from college and bought homes in Levittowns, jet planes began to take

---

* For the entrepreneurs reading this, add "monetization" to the list of innovative traits. If it doesn't generate new revenues at a profit, it's not true innovation.

over commercial aviation, and cars acquired larger tail fins. But it was still an age when parents and children listened to the same music, a family remained intact, the father was the sole breadwinner, and Loretta Young, keeping house in a dress and heels, was the avatar. You dressed for the party, the movie, or the rare restaurant dinner. Teachers were respected, and in every schoolroom the day started with a prayer and the Pledge of Allegiance. Youth received lessons in values at the family dinner table, in church, and at school.

Then came the '60s, when I went to Rutgers, and the world changed. The polio vaccine had arrived while I was still in high school (it was not unusual to have known people who died from polio); the inner cities burned; John Kennedy, Martin Luther King, and Bobby Kennedy were shot; the Cold War was in full swing; we landed on the moon after Sputnik scared the West; Vietnam claimed lives every day and spawned protests and sit-ins; the Cuban Missile Crisis was far scarier than any ISIS threat today; and the world seemed ruled by sex, drugs, and rock and roll. Music changed radically for youth; the Beatles appeared; Timothy Leary advised that we get high, tune in, and drop out; and hippies proliferated. Lenny Bruce kept getting arrested for a comedy act featuring obscenities that we now hear in popular music and on cable television. And you could still get a liberal arts education, a benefit all but extinct today. (See the epilogue.)

The '60s, for me, was the most exciting decade in my history. The shocks to the society of the '50s were tectonic. That's because the '50s were comparatively docile after World War II.

Today, we have an entirely different dynamic. We have to create change if we are to thrive.

I am well versed in problem solving, and for many years "quality" was paramount, with its black belts and "lean" Japanese words. But I found quickly that problem solving is a commodity, and not all that valuable, because we can do it well with a tight process.

But innovation is different. Innovation requires that we do not

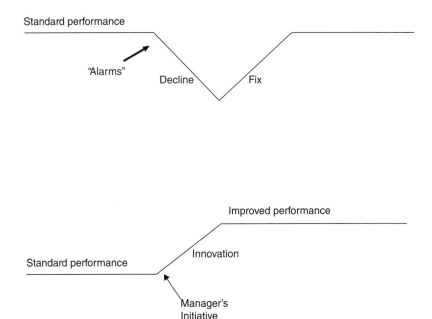

Figure 4.2: The Distinction of Innovation

seek relevant change, *but create relevant change.* That is, as you see in figure 4.2, we deliberately create a disruption. In fact, I was so sure of this, it became the subject of my first book, in 1988, which is still available for purchase (you're reading my sixtieth).* That book was part of the curriculum at the Wharton School, Temple University, and Villanova, and was translated into German and Italian. In fact, the former Italian premier, Silvio Berlusconi, wrote the foreword when he was CEO of Fiat, and we attracted scores of large clients.

I found that individuals and corporations were unduly bound by attempts to maintain the status quo or return poorer performance to

---

* *The Innovation Formula*, with Mike Robert: (Cambridge:Ballinger/Harper & Row, 1988).

its former state. But outstanding performers were trying to improve the status quo, just as the nonconformists of the '60s represented a breakthrough from the staid and complacent '50s. So we invented a methodical system of innovation, to augment the system of problem solving and give people more confidence.

There is more risk in innovation, but also far more reward. Even if you don't hit the height depicted in figure 4.2, you will still be better off than you were before. It's not my intent here to teach the steps of innovation—and you can read about them easily enough elsewhere—but rather to convey the importance of a volition to innovate. *Too many people think they are innovative when they are merely opportunistic.* This is a dangerous misconception.

If you were to find that taxis in your city were dirty and hard to find, and you launched a service that featured clean cars and better dispatching, you might succeed opportunistically and make money in a crowded market. But if you create Uber, you make a fortune in an entirely new market: on-demand, excellent transportation with safe, knowledgeable, and courteous drivers who speak English well.

You can form a new television network with distinctive programming and try to get audience share, or you can provide an entire season of a series at once, as Netflix has done, and create the phenomenon of binge watching.

You may try to convince your peers to accept your recommendations when a key decision is to be made, or you can create an environment where they actually experience the results of your decision. (Show me a working draft of a new website, don't merely tell me what you think is wrong with mine.)

The way to overcome volatility is to create your own positive and personal change. Instead of seeking the relevant change that caused a problem, create the relevant change that will improve your life.

When I was fired, I didn't attempt to find another job where I could perhaps be fired again. I started my own business, without experience or guidance in so doing. I named it, determined its focus, and told prospects that I was there (tell them you've built it or they won't come). I didn't try to "fix" anything, I started something new.

This is why almost all self-help books are deficient: they assume you're broken and try to fix you.

CHAPTER 5

Learning the Hard Way

Self-esteem, and lack thereof, is the monster under the bed. You can hear it in people's self-talk: "I shouldn't," "They'll question me," "It's not my place," "They'll never listen to me." Creating high self-esteem is a remedial skill, and one I've helped thousands to accomplish—and they thrive as a result.

We Should All Be Fired

I reported earlier that when I was abruptly fired by W. Clement Stone and called my wife from O'Hare Airport, she asked, "Well, what do you want to do now?"

I replied, "I want to work for myself so that no moron can ever fire me again."

"Okay," she said, "screw the mortgage, but you need to get *serious*."

When we were first married she warned me to always put the toothpaste cap back on the tube, and I've never missed. And I decided that I would also be unwaveringly true to the advice about getting serious. (I didn't actually feel it was "advice," so much as a commandment.)

This was one of those landmark events that many authorities believe happen a few times to very successful people. It was, perhaps, the rationalized happiness that Dan Gilbert at Harvard advocates, and/or the positive self-talk that Marty Seligman believes is integral to positive psychology.* Whatever it was, it worked.

When people face trauma, they become either distraught or angry. (Different from Elisabeth Kübler-Ross's five stages of grief: denial, anger, bargaining, depression, acceptance.†) I'm not referring to death and losses of loved ones, but to shocks to one's self-esteem. Being chastised publicly, being passed over for promotion, being fired, failing any kind of test, not being chosen to play in the game: these are all traumas of one degree or another.

When we allow these setbacks to depress us—to make us distraught—we lose the ability to cope. We wallow in self-pity and try to find those with whom we can commiserate. This is a waste of energy. We must all endure pain, but suffering is voluntary.

Mindsets: We often face unexpected, inescapable pain, but we create our own suffering.

Various religious and ethical systems tell us to "turn the other cheek," *but not one advocates that you allow yourself to continue to be struck.*

When we allow the natural anger to erupt and we deal with it, we no longer internalize it, blaming ourselves. I was fired by someone whose belief system was alien to mine and, I believed then and

---

* Dan Gilbert, *Stumbling on Happiness* (New York: Knopf, 2006); Martin Seligman, *Learned Optimism* (New York: Simon and Schuster, 2011).
† Elisabeth Kübler-Ross, *On Death and Dying* (New York: Macmillan, 1969).

now, deeply flawed. By directing my anger at what I saw as the source of my trauma, I could let it dissipate; I could then use that otherwise wasted energy to invest in my own improvement and success.

Not only was this a landmark event and an opportunity to realize that I should begin my own practice, it set a precedent for me in terms of future setbacks and trauma. By *believing* that getting fired was the best thing that ever happened to me, I was able to use it for fuel and solace instead of anger and resentment.

The real question is about directing your energy toward the positive, rather than allowing it to be drained or wasted.

Every disappointment that we allow to fester depletes our energy. This is often cumulative over a prolonged time period, because people don't properly rejuvenate each morning. They go to sleep fretting about a setback and wake up still obsessed with it. The question becomes, for all of us: Is each new day a great opportunity and chance to run (like my dogs) fearlessly through an open gate, or is it a long, slow, crawl through enemy territory?

Here are some immediately applicable lessons:

• Identify with your results, not your job title. I was asked to coach a vice chairman of an organization that was merging, so he was being asked to leave. He was given a nice severance package, which included my help in landing on his feet. He was only in his early fifties. But it was soon apparent that taking away his title had stripped him of his identity. He was accustomed to the status and automatic deference, and he had lost all self-regard. "How long before you can find me another vice chair or even chairman's position?" he asked when I met him. (I was reminded that in the 1940s and 1950s, many officers returning from the war were still referred to as "major" or "colonel" even in the insurance company or bank in which they found a new career or resumed an old one.)

- Do not generalize from a specific. At a certain point in time you did not get the sale, or the job, or the interview, or the assignment. That's it. There is no related commentary on your overall abilities, worth, or value. Compartmentalize the offense. Seal the watertight doors so that the leak doesn't sink the ship, and you can subsequently pump out the water.

- You will keep growing, as long as you seek sustenance. No matter how many times you mow the lawn, the grass will keep growing. It doesn't give up, doesn't take the hint, and often comes back stronger than ever. But the grass will die if it's deprived of water. Don't worry about the setback, but don't allow it to deny you of sustenance. Use friends and family, reserves and reallocations, and keep the nutrients flowing. Too many people embark on an inadvertent "hunger strike" when they hit a wall.

We should all be fired. We need the experience of deep disappointment and ambiguity about our futures. When I ask successful people in my speeches how many have been fired at least once, a minimum of half the room raises a hand.

"It's a great club, isn't it?," I ask, and they all smile.

It's the best thing that ever happened to me.

Not All Relationships Are Made in Heaven

From the Gospel of St. Mark (6:4): "A prophet is not without honor except in his native place and among his own kin and in his own house."

One of the things I learned the hard way is that relationships vary in duration, intensity, and meaning. We often try to preserve relationships at all costs, as if they are sacrosanct and inviolable.

They are not.

We make concessions regularly in the best relationships, and create unquestioning connections in the worst. The athletes who are fined, suspended, even fired—earning, at the time, millions of dollars but found guilty of ethical and/or legal lapses—are often still connected to relationships that should have been extinguished years earlier. Michael Vick, the talented professional quarterback, went to jail for organizing dogfighting bouts. He was still pals with childhood friends who hadn't outgrown their upbringing and adolescent experiences, and so he hadn't either.

I'll pose an uncomfortable question: In a world of perhaps six billion people, do you think that you found your current partner, spouse, or significant other because he or she was the *only* one for you? (I'm married for forty-seven years, so this isn't just an abstract theory.) If you had the option of searching for every conceivable partner in a dazzlingly short time frame—sort of nanosecond dating—would your current special person be the one? How about you who are divorced or separated? Obviously, the person you split from wasn't the perfect match.

There are others who will piously tell you to repair any and all broken (or poor) relationships in your family, because someday you will no longer be able to do so. Yet we don't choose our families, especially those aunts and cousins and nephews, so what's the big deal about ideal relationships?

What about your job or profession? Is it precisely right for you, or did you stumble into it? Did you inherit it from a parent, or were you forced into it by normative pressure? Is this what you would have chosen for yourself?

I've found clients and colleagues who live under the incredible rubric (and pressure) that relationships should be created, nurtured, and sustained, no matter what. It's as if a relationship is akin to washing your hair or using cutlery instead of your fingers—a social requisite beyond all doubt or reproach.

Well, it just ain't so. How pleasurable is it to argue with the same drunken uncle at every family event, or defend your career to a snide cousin who is not nearly as successful, or deal with your father, who claims you'll never amount to much, even though you're the CEO of a respected firm? (True story: It happened regularly to a client of mine who headed the American branch of a major international financial firm. His father said he had a "nothing" job, and it undermined his effectiveness and self-worth. Yet he wouldn't cut off communication.)

We need to sever relationships that no longer serve us well or, worse, actively undermine us. We need to create new relationships as our circumstances improve and change, and look at them as of finite duration. In our partners, we have found someone with whom we wish to forge a life together, and we haven't tried to empirically prove that person is the sole or best candidate. Long-term relationships are built not only on love, but on compromise, understanding, acceptance of hurt, acknowledgment of responsibility for mistakes, and so forth. That's what we do with someone we want to commit our lives to. It's not for everyone.

In business, my advice has always been true to what I've called the Michelangelo Factor. Having carved the exquisite *David* from a single, cast-off piece of marble, the sculptor was asked how he possibly could have conceived the result. (The piece is awe-inspiring, with veins in the legs and precise detail that would be impressive in a painting, let alone a sculpture.) "I carved away everything that didn't look like David," he purportedly replied. (If the story isn't true, it should be.) He culled, he didn't add.

We all need to find what we love to do—are passionate about—and are excellent at doing. We build our careers around that, not what our parents did or our friends suggest or some dumb paper test tells us we're cut out for. We need to *remove* from our careers, not add to them. Otherwise, Michelangelo would have created a statue too large, too busy, and too patched together.

There is no such thing as a "necessary evil." There *is* such a thing as self-imposed drudgery and metaphoric self-flagellation. If you don't enjoy spending four hours cutting the lawn, then hire some kid to do it (or a lawn service, if you're anal-retentive). If you don't like someone's company, stop feeling obligated to accept her invitations. If you don't like your career, change it. If you don't like your boss, move on. You think that's tough to do? I'll tell you what's tougher: surrendering eternally to others' wishes, others' objectives, others' demands—all at the expense of your own.

I read this from John Dewey years ago, and I'm guessing it's his original work, but it bears repeating nonetheless:

> Better it is for philosophy to err in active participation in the living struggles and issues of its own age and times than to maintain an immune monastic impeccability.... while saints are engaged in introspection, burly sinners run the world. *

It's far better for us, in our lives and in our work, to face the reality of relationships: they need to be altered, changed, abandoned, and created on an ongoing basis.

Not long ago, my wife and I attended our fiftieth high school reunion. It was nice seeing so many of the old crowd, and it was fun to reminisce. But no one is planning our fifty-fifth. There are no regrets that we gave up those relationships at the proper times.

---

* "Better it is for philosophy to err in active participation in the living struggles and issues of its own age and times than to maintain an immune monastic impeccability, without relevancy and bearing in generating ideas of its contemporary present" from "Does Reality Possess Practical Character?," 1908; "And while saints are engaged in introspection, burly sinners run the world" from *Reconstruction in Philosophy*, 1920.

Throwing Water on Personal Outrage

For a long time I advocated (and justified to myself daily) a "healthy, personal sense of outrage." This would be fine if we were talking about animal cruelty or the strange ways the Giants beat the Patriots in the Super Bowl, but it was an intense rationalization for taking personally the daily slights we all endure.

I had an eidetic memory for slights.

And I was angry most of the time. That sucks energy out of you like a vacuum cleaner working a dusty corner. Everything goes: dust, bugs, webs, lint, small change, and, perhaps, that college fraternity pin you'd been missing all these years.

Case Study

I know a woman who is perpetually angry. She is pugnacious, always ready (and actually looking) for a fight. She is highly defensive, blames others for her own woes, and will resort to ill-timed humor or blatant profanity to divert feedback.

She is functional and can work with clients, but is an absolute royal pain to be around. Her behavior is enabled because no one feels the need to suffer the kind of pain that's involved in trying to help someone who clearly doesn't want to be helped.

And the fuel for this anger will never otherwise diminish, because she is basically angry at herself.

We all know people who react to the person changing lanes without a directional signal or holding up the line in the bank while shooting the breeze with the teller as a personal slight. The person who stops stock still at the bottom of an escalator or pauses in the doorway to discuss the performance as the theater disgorges patrons is oblivious, rude, and clueless. But that person has not launched a vendetta against you specifically.

George Carlin used to do a comedy bit where he pointed out that the driver in front of you going so slowly is an idiot, and the driver tailgating you because you won't get out of the way is a moron. Too many of us see things in terms of a personal attack rather than a flaw manifested publicly by others.

A healthy personality can discriminate between those who are socially maladaptive and those who are singularly malicious. Someone cutting a line by twenty people is crude and unethical, but is treating *everyone* with the same contempt. Someone who tries to steal your tickets is a thief, and malicious.

You have to judge the other person's *intent*. Is the act that is driving you crazy specifically intended to harm you or to cause you discomfort, or are you merely caught in the wake of an inappropriate public act? Someone taking a cell phone call during a performance is stupid and selfish, and ruins the experience for everyone. But someone whose child cries on an airplane would prefer the child behave well, and probably is exhausting every effort to correct the situation.

Mindsets: Ask yourself what the other person's motive probably is. Is it really to strike at you, personally?

Intent is especially important in relationships. If your spouse or partner (or date) critiques the restaurant, or suggests the car be washed, or doesn't put the cap back on the toothpaste, is it an act motivated by the wish to hurt you or drive you mad? Or is it just a legitimate request, or an unexpected or ill-timed one, or none of the above? We tend to connect unpleasant feedback or behavior with personal attacks even when, most of the time, no such motive is extant.

The same holds true in our working relationships. Consultants walk in the door, listen to the prospect, and assume he is the cause of the problem, *despite the fact that he was smart enough to contact the consultants for help!* Our boss makes a decision and we convince ourselves that it's not good for us because the boss has it in for us, because of some innocuous comment made in a meeting because . . . It never ends.

It's as if you think your neighbor might borrow your lawnmower, and you believe he wouldn't return it, and that upsets you—so the next time you see your neighbor you're less than cordial because you're thinking *if* he borrowed your lawnmower—which he hasn't—he wouldn't return it! This is the kind of personal outrage that drowns talent, depletes energy, and ruins relationships (and potential).

You have to drench your pent-up sense of outrage with common sense. Neither the world nor the government nor random people you encounter are out to get you. You may not like the tax system, but it wasn't designed to torture you, personally. (You may win the lottery, by the way, but it, too, wasn't designed to help you, personally.)

There is a paranoia that pervades the worldview of some people, who are convinced there are conspiracies against them and that others are keeping secrets from them. That pertains to air force hangars in the desert purportedly housing crashed aliens, attempts by the United Nations to take over the government, and illnesses that are deliberately being spread (or allowed to go untreated) among certain people. The paranoid believe in conspiracies because it's the only way to explain why others can't understand their reasoning.*

---

* The idea that the government can keep secrets for years, despite regularly being hacked and secrets being leaked, is beyond belief.

Here's how to throw water on the smoldering embers of burning outrage:

- Always ask yourself what the motive of the behavior is and whether it was aimed specifically at you. This is especially crucial in personal relationships.

- Join a group if you feel the cause is just and represented by levelheaded people. It's smart to organize and lobby for tax reform, but it's suicidal to evade taxes personally, and it's simply insane to argue that the Constitution doesn't really demand that people pay taxes. (Plan to pave your own roads?)

- Assess the real harm done. The person breaking into the line isn't going to take your seat or cause you to be unable to get in. The driver who cuts you off isn't going to ruin your trip unless you engage in road rage and follow him several exits past yours. Saying "excuse me" will almost always move someone out of your way.

- Use my favorite New York phrase: fuggedaboudit. It's no big deal. Do you want to spend your time and energy being constantly enraged? *Is that what you want your kids (or coworkers or friends) to see?* Unless you follow a gnat home to find out where it lives and destroy its origins, stop obsessing. And if you do perform that pursuit, nothing I say here is helpful to you and you're probably already outraged.

We all often engage in *recency bias*. We are impacted and influenced by what happened to us most recently. If that's outrage, we become tinderboxes of anger, and we tend to explode or act precipitously. That means the oaf who cut you off prompts an overreaction with your family, and the inconsiderate colleague who cuts off your presentation in a meeting engenders a fight with a colleague later on. Throw water—douse yourself—when you feel the onset of what I call "life rage" and run the risk of a disproportionate response to an inevitable vicissitude. Can you accept that without getting upset?

Self-Esteem Must Be Built Daily

Remember my story about being chosen as an exchange student? While the countries I visited and people I met were dazzling, I was also learning how to improve my self-esteem, though I didn't realize it at the time.

My colleague from Finland, Esko, and I would sneak up from cabin class (second class) on the original *Queen Mary* to wander around the first-class dining room, theater, pool, and so on. And we would be tossed out continually (there were two crew members for every passenger, as I recall). We were literally—physically—thrown out by the ship's crew. For five days we made these forays and for five days we were removed forcibly.

On the channel steamer from England to France, our tickets were so cheap that we were only allowed on the open deck. It was nighttime and freezing. Our reporter/chaperone found a heating grate to sleep on, but the two of us tried to crash first class once again. And we were thrown out into the cold all night. At one point we were thrown *up* a staircase and out a door!

We stayed in youth hostels and cheap hotels throughout Europe, and crowded into a Volkswagen Beetle for much of the trip. And here's the lesson I appreciated far later.

Neither of us ever resented getting tossed out of places *or the people who rightfully occupied those places*. Instead, we agreed to live that way ourselves someday, and we did. We didn't opt for anarchy or nihilism; we didn't want revenge or retribution. We simply wanted to deserve what they deserved by working for it and applying our talents.

A few years ago, I booked the most expensive suite on the seas: the aft, bi-level, 2,500-square-foot "stateroom" on the *Queen Mary II*. We had a sweeping staircase, a butler, a huge balcony, our own reserved table at any hour in the dining room, and every convenience. It cost $50,000. But I knew some day I'd do it. The same applies to my lifestyle and accomplishments. I've never envied anyone anything or felt I had to have what they have *unless it made sense for me.*

Here is what I live by: TIAABB. There is always a bigger boat.

The sultan of Brunei and Paul Allen may vie for a few extra feet on their next new $200-million yachts, but who cares? They can't dock them in most harbors and most people will never see those yachts. If that's what makes them happy, fine, but the rowboat on our pond is all I want to handle.

Too many people seek entitlements. They want something simply because others have it, not because they have earned it. The worst thing to do with an entitlement mentality is to enable it. Giving people something for nothing—unless they are truly incapable

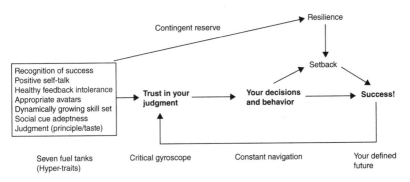

Figure 5.1: Trusting Your Judgment

of acquiring basic needs—may enrich their temporary condition, but it impoverishes their spirit.

The basic issue with self-esteem is the ability to trust one's judgment.

I've found that most people don't trust their own judgment, so they tend to trust *other people's judgment*, which may be entirely wrong for them (or lousy, period). Or they use trial and error, an extremely expensive and risky means to make decisions about their lives.

You see on the left of figure 5.1 what I consider the keys to building trust in your own judgment:

1. Recognition of success: Knowing what constitutes success for you. Hint: It should never be perfection, but "merely" the attainment of important goals.

2. Positive self-talk: You should start and end the day with the positives in your life, what you intend to accomplish and what you have accomplished.

3. Healthy feedback intolerance: Don't listen to people you haven't asked, because unsolicited feedback *is almost always for the sender's benefit.* This conflicts with the "humility school" people who tell you *all* feedback is good feedback. It isn't. Listen only to those you trust and whom *you ask.*

4. Appropriate avatars: Whom do you admire? What traits are important? Everyone talks about Steve Jobs's wonderful stewardship at Apple, but he was a terrible person, husband, and father.

5. Dynamically growing skill sets: Confidence in judgment is buoyed by rising competence in diverse areas.

6. Social cue adeptness: You should be able to recognize when to speak and when to listen, which requests are appropriate and inappropriate, and when to offer help and when to mind your own business.

7. Judgment: As Thomas Jefferson is often said to have observed, "In matters of taste, swim with the tide, in matters of principle, stand like a rock."

Your judgment will then lead to better decisions and behavior to achieve your defined future (success), and also serve as a contingent reserve when you experience a setback and need the resilience to bounce back and not be defeated.

I call the seven traits "hyper-traits," and the trust in your own judgment your personal gyroscope, which keeps you on balance, upright, and headed in the right direction.

Self-esteem is like a muscle, and it should be developed on a regular basis or it will atrophy. You can't attend a boot camp or sit in a sweat tent or trod hot coals to gain self-esteem. (In fact, many psychologists report that patients come to them after these experiences, frustrated that there is no connection to their daily life and success.) You need to gain tangible skills and engage in the proper self-talk.

George Carlin observed that, if you're reading a book, it's not "self-help." He had a point. I never assume, in writing this, that you're damaged or deficient. I'm simply relating those areas where I needed to improve, how I did so, and what resulted.

Mindsets: You need a self-esteem workout on a regular basis and, just as with a physical workout, you may need a trainer or coach to help you.

I continue to review my successes and build my self-esteem daily. There are other people who are trying constantly to knock us down or undermine us or throw us out the door.

Don't get angry. Get what you need to be successful on your own terms.

Case Study

I had keynoted the opening of the convention of the Professional Speaking Association in Birmingham, England. There was a reception afterward, and I couldn't get out of it since the crowd washed me onto its shore.

Sure enough, a "speech coach" cornered me and asked if I'd like some feedback on my talk. I asked him if there was anything left in what remained of the British Empire that could stop him. He ignored my request.

"When you move around the stage," he continued, "I can't focus on the points you're making. But when you stand in one place (he planted his feet solidly in demonstration) I can focus on your points. Do you know what this is called?"

"Yes," I assured him, "a learning disability."

CHAPTER 6

Pain, Not Suffering

My early "success" involved shooting everyone in the room, then asking if they could support my position. Then I learned that there was always someone with heavier artillery, and that allies were the key to success. We need to understand and apply the principles of leveraged support and convince others that "the road less traveled" is less traveled because it's an inferior road.

Compartmentalizing Pain

Facebook displays more public grief than any other media platform, in my experience. We see photos of injured people, of people in hospital beds with tubes and wires attached, and of deceased relatives, as well as memorials to former pets and so forth. Private grief has given way to a public rending of garments, virtually.

We are all faced with pain. Some of us face it professionally and institutionally—hospice workers, surgeons, police officers, therapists (to name a few). Yet most of these people are able to endure, despite seeing death, assisting those in great pain, and counseling those in grief. They don't absorb the pain they encounter, nor the suffering; otherwise, who could do their jobs? I've always been surprised that a clinician, hearing generally woes and regrets for forty hours a week, can still drive home devoid of road rage and engage in dinner conversation about her daughter's soccer game or son's music recital.

In most holy books, there's an admonition to "turn the other cheek." We may hear it in a sermon or from a parent in response to a hurt that was inflicted by someone else. And it's true that a visceral reaction to being struck or hurt is often ill advised. After all, sometimes the hurt is inadvertent.

But nowhere in any tract or proverb that I've read or heard are we advised to turn the other cheek *and allow ourselves to continue to be hit*. We can deal with the pain the first time, but we needn't submit ourselves to ongoing suffering.

Pain is unavoidable. Suffering is not.

We undergo pain, often unpreventable. But suffering is a decision, a choice, a measured response.

I was always skeptical of wakes. I recall a classmate who had a serious heart condition so severe that he couldn't participate in games and had purple lips. Finally, halfway through high school, it was determined that an operation was necessary and he was thought to be ready. He died on the operating table.

When a group of us attended the very Italian wake, I was astounded at the public grieving, crying, and lamentations that went on. But I realized later that this was the "appointed suffering" stage, where we all joined in the pain and the mutual support, family and friends. Jews sit shiva for the same purposes. After the prescribed period of suffering, we are to get back to our lives. Some of us, of course, choose to continue to suffer. That is a choice, not a biologic requirement. That sounds harsh, perhaps, but it's true.

I love dogs and have, therefore, lost dogs to age and illness. It's horrible; their lives are too short. But my response is to honor their deaths and then acquire more dogs to continue in their spirit, and that's the advice I've given to countless people who have come to me in the same condition. Suffering doesn't help. The pain must be dealt with, but it's never the pain that lasts, it's the self-imposed suffering.

I've encountered people who, years later, decry their not choosing a lottery number on a certain day, bemoan the relationship they allowed to attenuate, complain about the poor deal they received from someone else, or regret the job assignment they didn't pursue or accept. It is a litany of suffering that benumbs the spirit and saps all energy.

> **Mindsets:** Your suffering is a conscious choice that shouldn't be seen as a requirement or unavoidable condition.

We need to compartmentalize pain; otherwise, it seeps into every crevice of our existence. Our missing a promotion at work shouldn't lessen our enjoyment of our children's accomplishments at school. A bad argument at home can't affect our judgment in evaluating a subordinate's performance on the job.

If we don't compartmentalize pain, we allow it to surface and to fuel anger in inappropriate settings. You don't want to scream obscenities at the cop who pulled you over because your spouse said vile things at breakfast, and you don't want to explode at your boss after you found out that the vet can't do anything for your pet.

It's not a matter of other people not understanding your pain (though they often don't), but it is a matter of their perception of how you deal with suffering ("Would you please step out of the car?"; "I don't know if he can deal with the pressures of leading the western office").

This is my advice to you if you want to control pain and reduce suffering to be highly successful:

- Allow yourself to suffer for a given period and to a given degree, but not uncontrollably.

- Replace what was lost with a new pursuit or interest or relationship.
- Tell people you trust about your pain, but do not inflict your suffering. And don't allow them to do so either.
- Don't grieve publicly (that is, among strangers and virtual acquaintances). It actually demeans your pain by making it a spectacle.

Life is far too diverse and unpredictable to avoid pain and suffering, but we can compartmentalize the pain and limit the suffering so that we can be resilient and energetic, and escape long-term depression.

Generalizing Victories

I once managed international sales forces. Because I was trained to search for distinctions, I was constantly asking, "What's distinctive about the best performers compared with the next best?" What I found, among the obvious traits (high self-esteem, enthusiasm, and so forth), was the ability to generalize from a specific positive and isolate specific negatives.

If most of us try to play an instrument unsuccessfully, we generalize that negative: I have no affinity for music. But what's actually occurred is that you couldn't learn how to play the piano at age twenty with that particular instructor amidst the other obligations and time pressures of that period. (Originally, I feared speaking in public, and now I'm among the fewer than 1 percent of all speakers in the Speaker Hall of Fame.)

I've heard poor salespeople say things like:

Maybe I'm not cut out for sales.
This new product can't be sold.

The customers are getting tired of the offerings.

You're not giving me the same support I used to get. (I loved that one!)

They were generalizing from a single negative experience, or even several. But what they were creating was their own "doom loop": I didn't sell this, I'm not very good at sales, the next person I visit will realize it, I didn't make that sale either, I'm not very good at this, the next person...

The best people talked like this:

I can sell anything.

I love to face new objections.

People can't resist me.

I'm going to set new records.

This isn't merely about being "positive," though I've discussed the power and importance of that already. It's about the ability to generalize from a specific success to general success. In this case, you learn to play the piano and say, "I can master any instrument I choose to."

You create an "achievement loop": I sold this over tough objections, I can overcome any objection, the next person I see will experience this, that person bought, I'm constantly overcoming objections, the next person will experience this, I sold to that person...

The occasional setback becomes an aberration in an achievement loop, but the occasional victory *becomes "luck" in the doom loop.*

Mindsets: You establish your loop. You often require help to break the doom loop and enter the achievement loop.

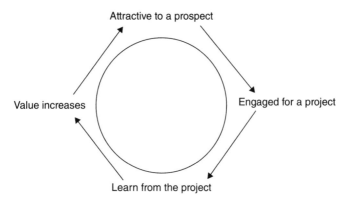

Figure 6.1: A Sales Achievement Loop

When I realized I could successfully speak in front of tough high school assemblies, I realized I could speak anywhere—not just in that high school before those groups, and not just at seventeen, and not just in that city. I realized that what I was doing wasn't luck because I was able to constantly replicate it.

In figure 6.1 you can see a sample achievement loop for a salesperson. You prove yourself attractive to a prospect, you win the business, you learn from the experience (replicate success), your value as a resource increases, and you become even more attractive to the next prospect. This is all based on refusing to see singular or isolated successes as one-time (or, worse, *random*) events, but rather as indications of how genuinely good you are.

Figure 6.2 shows the doom loop for a sales professional, which no amount of training will solve or improve. This is a coaching challenge, helping people generalize from specific achievements rather than setbacks.

I'm convinced that the prime differentiator between those who are in pain because of presumed failings and engage in endless suffering and those who are free of pain and engaged in continuing victories is the ability to generalize single successes into lifelong beliefs about worth.

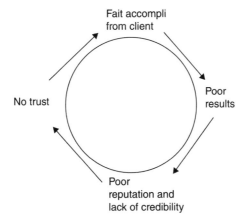

Figure 6.2: The Doom Loop

Bill Buckner was an excellent ballplayer for the Boston Red Sox, but his entire athletic history has been reduced to the ball that went through his legs while he was playing first base in the sixth game of the 1986 World Series against the New York Mets. The Red Sox would have won the series, but that error allowed the Mets to win game six, and they went on to win the seventh game and the championship.

Buckner should never have been in the game. He was injured, and there was an excellent defensive replacement available late in the game, but the manager chose to leave Buckner in "to experience the glory of winning the series" and that proved to be a horrible decision. Despite his career with three teams (he had set records as a first baseman) that single error was generalized into his overall evaluation. People still talk about it in Boston. (I'm sure they're saying similar things in Seattle about the Patriots winning the Super Bowl in 2015, when Seahawks coach Pete Carroll called for a pass that was intercepted on the goal line at the end of the game, though they had the best runner in the game available and just two yards to go for the winning touchdown and second consecutive Super Bowl title.)

We can't allow ourselves to be defined—especially by ourselves—by a single error or some poor choices. We have to define ourselves by our success and achievement, and that success and achievement can be a single instance that fuels future ones. One of the counterintuitive points I found is that generalizing victories often relies on the *subordination* of ego.

Subordinating Ego

I discussed earlier, with only mild hyperbole, my technique for gaining consensus: shoot first, ask politely later. I belonged to a consulting firm in Princeton where this was the rule (picture *Mad Men* on steroids), and we practiced the quick draw rather than the consummate argument. Argument was for debate teams, and didn't those go out with Latin?

In figure 6.3 you can see a representation of something I realized once I was licking my wounds, counting my scars, and notching my guns. Every organization—and person—has only 100 percent of talent and energy to expend. The old rubrics and apothegms about "giving 110 percent" belong in dated movies about Notre Dame football or admonitions from some motivational guru who's asked that you build sand castles on the beach at high tide.

That energy and talent is applied either externally or internally. Period.

For the organization:

Internal is office gossip, turf battles, concerns about job security, desires for promotion, an attractive coworker, the poor food in the vending machines, the boring boss.

External is the client or customer, the product, service, and relationship.

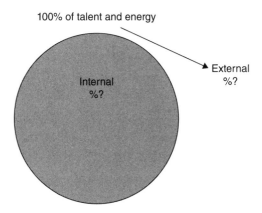

Figure 6.3: Where Is the Energy Going?

For the individual:

Internal is self-doubt, self-limiting beliefs, paranoia, low self-esteem, concerns about health, hidden aspirations, stress.

External is the family, career, contributions to society, philanthropy, new experiences.

I learned that we must subordinate ego to truly create an external focus professionally and personally. It occurred to me at long last that meeting my critical objectives was far more important than triumphing over others at every opportunity. I didn't need the best office, only a good one; I didn't require 100 percent unanimity, just enough support to achieve my purpose. I learned that consensus is something you can live with, not something you die for.

Mindsets: If you put your ego on the bow of the ship, it's going to get whacked by waves until it's unrecognizable.

We often suffer the most when we lead with our egos. You can see the person in the meeting who tries to get the "right" answer before all others in front of the boss, or who cuts off colleagues to suggest her solution first. I have a strong ego, in the sense that I'm very confident and am not intimidated in any business or social situation. But *I've learned to allow my presence to speak for itself, rather than speaking to demonstrate that I'm present.*

Here's what I mean: I meet some people who immediately tell me, on any pretext at all, that they were quoted in the *New York Times* or that they're just back from Venice or that they once understudied on Broadway. It's their opening salvo—the same as me drawing my guns in the old days, trying to "wow" the other person immediately to establish superiority. Yet it's far more powerful to simply comment during conversations using your experience and learning.

"The *David* is breathtaking, we were fortunate to get to Firenze to see it a year ago."

"I agree with you about Far Niente and Heitz Cellars, what other big California red wines do you favor?"

As I mentioned, you're reading my sixtieth book. An overbearing woman was introduced at dinner the other night, a relative of one of my best clients, and she regaled me with her accomplishments. When she asked me what I did, I said, "I write a little." She said, "How nice, have you ever actually written a book?"

"Yes," I said, "more books on consulting than anyone in history." She was quite subdued after that.*

This chapter is about pain, not suffering, and I'm addressing it here in a slightly different way. It's painful to continually argue with people, and you *will* be made to suffer, if they can manage it, at some future point. (It's tough to refuse the suffering imposed by relatives or bosses.) If you subordinate your ego—don't forsake it or

---

* The story goes that the great dancer Fred Astaire's original audition card read, "Thin voice, balding, dances a little."

deny it, merely subordinate it in the moment—you'll have a totally different approach to gaining influence or even denying influence to others who don't merit it.

I knew I had "made it" when I didn't constantly have to prove myself to others. In many cases, colleagues do this for you, extolling your accomplishments for those unfamiliar with you in a kind of social evangelism. But in most instances, your presence is sufficient: knowing when to interject and when to accept, when to suggest and when to merely approve.

I was waiting to speak at an event with about two hundred people, sitting at a table in the rear of the room. The woman next to me looked at my initials monogrammed on my shirt cuff, and the same initials on my pen, and my name on my briefcase. She looked at me and said quite innocently, "Are you afraid you'll forget who you are?"

Just like my erstwhile insistence on initials, persistence in informing people how good we are, seeking to win every single point, and trying to parade our superiority is not the way to gain wealth, and it's certainly not the way to achieve any kind of accomplishment without stress. But I feel that many people who begin anything by telling you how good they are or how much they have are displaying initials—trying to remind themselves who they are in their own image of themselves.

But it's only the image seen by others that matters.

You don't want to discourage children by never allowing them to win at a card game or checkers or tic-tac-toe. You don't want to discourage a partner by always cooking something better than he does or taking a better photo, or dancing a tango.

Organizations need to subordinate corporate ego (banks, phone companies, and cable operations are justifiably considered arrogant and uncaring) as much as people need to subordinate personal ego.

If my wife and I hadn't subordinated our egos at the right times (at least most of the time) we wouldn't have made it for forty-seven days, let alone forty-seven years.

Afflict the Comfortable; Comfort the Afflicted

Thus far I've been discussing your pain and your suffering, with the first largely involuntary and the second mostly voluntary. We all experience pain—physical and mental—but we inflict suffering on ourselves, *sometimes for a lifetime.*

But what about how we affect others?

James Carville, the brilliant political analyst and operative, was my guest not long ago at my annual Thought Leadership Conference. He has insights into political creatures such as I've never heard, especially over some fine Maker's Mark bourbon. He told a fascinating story when asked why Bill Clinton has such charisma and charm.

Carville related that when Bill Clinton walked into a room— as candidate, president, visitor, guest, whatever—he made it a habit to seek out a person he thought was the most uncomfortable, the lowest "ranking," the most unlikely to be invited, and immediately strike up a conversation. Carville pointed out that anyone in the room would have dropped whatever they were doing to have the limelight shining on them in speaking with Clinton, but instead he directed attention to the person who needed some confidence and, perhaps, some glory.

I think this is a marvelous practice. I belong to the National Speakers Association, and am in their Speaker Hall of Fame. I belong to the Institute of Management Consultants and have been named a fellow, one of only two people in history with both credentials. As a result, we receive all kinds of initials to use after our names, different color name tags, different seating, and so on, and on, and on. If I wanted, my business card or signature line could look like this:

Alan Weiss, PhD, CSP, CMC, CPAE, FCMC

That and a couple of bucks might get me on a bus.

And this is the way people treat each other, with these tribal signs of hierarchy. It's as if a lack of initials makes you unintelligent, non-sentient. There are actually people I encounter with two dozen or more stupefying and idiotic initials after their names, all hieroglyphics, all ego driven and vain. When I mentioned this once on Twitter, twenty people left in a huff, all trailing indecipherable initials behind them.

I'm afflicting the comfortable.

The title of this segment derives from early descriptions of Jesus: he comforted the afflicted and afflicted the comfortable. It's never my intent to cause people pain, but sometimes, I do merely by pointing out the folly in their habits or the nonsense in their reasoning. The suffering they endure is usually a function of whether they continue to combat the argument or insist on converting me to their way of thinking, or whether they can accept other points of view with open-mindedness and lack of threat to their own egos.

Being a contrarian, maverick, or provocateur means that you generally upset the apple cart and rock the boat. (As I write this, the news headline is that former Tour de France champion Greg LeMond is claiming some racers hid small motors in their bikes!) We are going to cause disturbance, disruption, and discontinuities. The productive key to all this is to do so with improvement in mind, and not destruction or vengeance. If you think back to my earlier example of "shooting" everyone in a meeting and then asking, "Shall we do it my way?" you'll see that the disruption is not positive and is meant to create pain *and* suffering.

I've grown. I think!

Mindsets: We endure pain; we create suffering—for ourselves and for others.

Comforting the Afflicted

As in Bill Clinton's case, we encounter people at work and in our lives who are "afflicted": with guilt, fear, envy, low self-esteem, a persecution complex, and so on. Sometimes they are simply afraid to speak up, tentative about their ideas. I believe we have to give them permission and even courage.

When I facilitate groups, I make it a habit to call on people from whom we've heard very little or nothing at all. I make sure I get back to people on phone conferences who tried to say something but were overrun by more assertive colleagues. I will poll groups to ensure that everyone has an opportunity to speak.

If we don't engage in this dynamic, we lose important insights, creativity, and ideas. There is zero correlation between volume and intelligence (as I can attest from the oaf sitting next to me at the bar last night loudly proclaiming that New Mexico is the only place to go to escape northern winters. Right, if you're a prairie dog.).

One of the most powerful techniques in your arsenal is drawing out people who have trouble emerging from their own cones of silence and, often, terror.

Afflicting the Comfortable

Sed quis custodiet ipsos custodes? (Who shall guard us from the guardians?) Juvenal raised that issue millennia ago, and it's a good question even today.

There are far too many people who are self-satisfied and smug.

Definitions

Confidence: The honest belief that you can help other people.

Arrogance: The belief that you have nothing more to learn yourself.

Smugness: Arrogance without the talent.

Who are these people? And why should we afflict them instead of merely ignoring them?

• They are so self-absorbed that they suck up all the oxygen in the room, demanding things for themselves without considering others. One person is cold and wants the temperature for the room changed without checking with the other thirty people sitting there.

• They not only have their own opinions, they have their own "facts." They will tell you that money will take care of motivation and complaints, yet research shows that money isn't a motivator, while reward from the work itself is.

• They have a poverty mentality that they wish to foist on others. Let's buy cheap seats and sneak up to better, vacant ones during the game. Let's buy cheap tickets and talk the gate agent into upgrading us.

• They insist that they prevail in matters of taste, not just principle. "Why would you go to that restaurant, I have a much better place we can go."

Case Study

A woman boarded the Acela high-speed train's first-class car one August in Providence. She was wearing a tiny pair of shorts, strappy sandals, and a midriff blouse with no sleeves. After a few minutes she complained to the first-class steward that she was cold.

The man told her he'd go adjust the air conditioning. The train car was comfortable, there were fifteen other people in the car, and the temperature outside was in the nineties.

"If you change the temperature just for her, I'll file a complaint!" I joked with the steward.

"Oh, I won't change a thing," he said, "I'll just walk to the back and pretend that I have."

When he returned, he asked the woman if the temperature were better.

"Oh, much better," she assured him.

A Million Dollar Maverick mindset calls for us not just to rock the boat but, occasionally, to capsize it. It's our duty to help those who need others' courage and insights, and to muffle those who think someone died and left them in charge.

CHAPTER 7

The Art of the Setup

We can stage-manage and choreograph our careers. I was a "prisoner" working in some firms, but I also found that many people who are refugees from corporations and start their own entrepreneurial companies are now working for a tougher boss! We are able to shape our own lives and businesses, our relationships and interactions. Our choice is to learn the steps or simply follow while someone else leads—not much of a choice.

If You Don't Blow Your Own Horn, There Is No Music

There is a truly damaging philosophy embraced by many that undermines their careers and subtly dampens their lives. Its colloquial name is "humility."

We are inculcated from a very early age *not* to stand out. We're told to stand in line and be quiet. (In my grammar school we were actually marked for "comportment," which generally stopped me from gaining straight As, yet I wound up speaking professionally as part of my career.) We are told not to brag, boast, or otherwise call attention to ourselves. I have no idea why. The admonition isn't

Biblical, or even practical. The star performers today—in athletics, entertainment, business, politics, medicine, law—all call attention to themselves. Exhibit A would be Donald Trump.

Let's go down that list, and you can fill in contemporary examples:

Athletics: Aaron Rodgers
Entertainment: Lady Gaga
Business: Donald Trump
Politics: Bernie Sanders
News: Brian Williams
Medicine: Dr. Oz
Law: Any personal injury lawyer

These people make or appear in commercials, appear on talk shows, and continually expand and diversify their brands. It's not always salutary: Dr. Oz went from distinguished heart surgeon to purveyor of questionable homeopathic medicines, and Brian Williams went from network news anchor to oblivion when he forgot his basic profession in trying to become a "personality," exaggerating and lying in the attempt.

I watched people who stood out in the organizations for which I consulted early in my career, people who were mentioned by others, and those who may not have had extraordinarily more talent but who gained the most mileage for the fuel they had. (In my list above, you can substitute others with less fame and just as much, if not more, talent.)

These are the traits I found that I could insert into a pattern, which I then emulated:

1. You have make your own accomplishments known. By all means give credit to others who helped, but unless you

---

Case Study

I once worked quite a bit in the Philippines, while managing our consulting firm's Asian operations. I was astonished the first time I visited lounges and bars in Manila in that there were outstanding musicians and singers playing American music. I don't mean good, I mean outstanding.

Then I found in the United States that there were groups doing theater in Dallas or performing in Charlotte that were as good as anything in the movies or on Broadway. Occasionally, they are "discovered": *August: Osage County*, first performed by the Steppenwolf Theatre in Chicago, made it to Broadway and collected several Tony Awards. But that's uncommon.

Why are so many talented and devoted people unable to make it to the front ranks, while contemporaries or even mediocre people pass them by?

---

blow your own horn in this manner, someone else will be assigned credit for it. (In the middle of a huge scrum trying to rebound a basketball, at five-feet-ten-inches, I came down with the ball and put it in the basket, but the scorers couldn't see me and gave the two points to a taller guy they could see. I never told them it was I.)

Mindsets: Credit never goes unclaimed. If you don't take credit someone else will, no matter how much it belongs to you. The lottery ticket you stuck in the back of the drawer will be gone, cashed by someone else.

2. Make your case with people who matter. In consulting, I interacted frequently with the economic buyer (the investor in the project) and didn't closely associate myself with gatekeepers such as human resources or purchasing. You must speak up at meetings, public or private, and make your voice heard as one of intelligence and reason.

3. Push back. Powerful and influential people are surrounded by a chorus of people singing "Yes" and "Brilliant" and "We're with you." To stand out, you need to clearly be your own best counsel and fearlessly resist jumping on bandwagons.

4. Look the part. I was never impressed by people trying hard to be herd members (every banker looks alike to me; they're afraid to look any other way). The converse, which creates the same result, is the "conventionally unconventional," who are actually the most conformist of all. I laugh involuntarily every time I see adults with a baseball cap on backward having to shield their eyes from the sun. I'm impressed by people with a sense of style appropriate to their position and singular self-image.

Humility is fine for the clergy, perhaps, but I find the most effective sermons come from people who are forceful and confident. Modesty may be fine for therapists, but the outstanding ones I've encountered haven't been afraid to give me their opinion and not just ask me, "How do you feel about that?"*

Life is competitive. You may choose not to compete, of course, but that leaves you on the sidelines, the player who sees action when

---

* Case in point: As I noted earlier, one of the most important, growth-oriented pieces of advice I ever received was from a therapist for $120 per fifty-five-minute session: "Alan, life is about success, not perfection." You'll find that theme throughout this book and most of my other ones.

the contest is already decided one way or another. You don't get to play while the game is still on the line. You don't make a difference unless you're in the game, and even then you have to swing the bat or call for the ball.

There is nothing wrong with making your talents and contributions manifest. (Remember my definitions of confidence, arrogance, and smugness in the previous chapter.) Most of you reading this are not in the clergy and you're not therapists. You may not be playing for the Yankees, the Canadiens, the Heat, Manchester United, or the Patriots. But you are able to play for yourself, in your life, in your field, in your way.

I've noted that Damon Runyon observed (in paraphrasing Ecclesiastes) that "the race is not always to the swift, nor the battle to the strong, but that's the way to bet." But there are a great many strong and a great many swift, and we tend to bet on emotional favorites and root for them to win. We also like to bet against the odds.

What I've just described is betting on yourself. You don't need to be the absolute strongest, just strong, or the absolute swiftest, just swift. But you do need to deliberately and diligently let other people know that.

The race is to those who blow their own horn while they run.

Shameless Promotion

Shameless promotion is the methodical and ongoing application of "blowing your own horn." It ensures music every day from a large and harmonious orchestra.

I can sell most people better than they can sell themselves. I run this exercise all the time. I ask a person what he does, and I'm told, "I'm a consultant who helps manufacturing companies control costs." After I ask a few questions, I create this introduction:

Please meet Stuart Jonas, who is a national expert on dramatically improving profits in manufacturing operations. His three degrees, work in six countries, forty published articles, and forthcoming book demonstrate why you can't afford to pass up the opportunity to work with him if his schedule permits.

Hyperbole? Not really. It's all true, though boldly and imaginatively stated. The six countries include the U.S., the forthcoming book is not yet sold to a publisher, and two of his degrees are in English literature—but I told you this was "shameless."

For many years I've hosted a Million Dollar Club at exotic locales around the world. One year, in Monaco, I met for the first time the husband of a woman who was a charter member. As we shook hands and sat in the lounge he said, "I've been looking forward to meeting you. What's your story?"

"Oh, it's a long story," I assured him, "and most people aren't interested." (That's because they're only interested in themselves.)

"I have plenty of time," he said, "I want to hear it all."

He went on to tell me that he starts most conversations with new people that way as a combination icebreaker and learning opportunity. And, of course, it also provides him the chance to talk about himself when you must reciprocate and ask him his story.

Case Study

I was conducting a session with newspaper editors at the American Press Institute. My focus was on helping them to use their live experiences to promote themselves both with their newspaper and with the public with whom they interacted.

Once I assigned the exercise (you'll see parts of it below), I noted one woman just staring at her keyboard. When I asked people to contribute their stories, she told me that she "had no story."

"Where did you go to school?"

"West Point."

"West Point?!" I calculated her age and years. "You must have been in one of the first classes to accept women."

"It was the very first."

"How did that go?"

"I was made first captain."

"That's the highest student rank, responsible for four thousand other students, right?"

"Yes, but then I just went into the army when I graduated."

"What was your specialty?"

"I became a paratrooper."

The rest of the class was spellbound by this woman "with no story." Oh, yeah, today she's a Carmelite nun.

Here are the questions to ask yourself to develop your "story" and to keep reminding yourself you're someone special, unique, and able to provide tremendous value to others. Take a few minutes to fill in the blanks or return to this later in the day when you have time:

1. What are your degrees in and where did you go to school?*

---

* Note that all answers are useful. If you never graduated from high school, that's quite a story given what you're doing today. There are no poor responses.

2. Where have you traveled?

_____

_____

3. What has been your greatest professional success?

_____

_____

4. What has been your greatest personal success?

_____

_____

5. What are your special abilities (musical instrument, athletics, hobbies, art)?

_____

_____

6. What awards, honors, special recognition have you received?

_____

_____

7. Cite an instance when you've coached someone, formally or informally, to great success.

_____

_____

You can see that you have quite a story to tell. You need to choose the most effective aspects of it for your purposes: to create an aura and presence so that people think about you. Whether for business purposes or personal pursuits, you want to become an object of interest to whom others are attracted.

So if you don't want to follow someone else's lead, if you don't want to be a part of the herd, you have to stand out. That process must begin with you. Ironically, once you've established your singular position, it is often propagated by others. How else can one explain the Kardashians?*

It's simple to use language to draft your particular promotional intentions. I can tell you that my wife drives a seven-year-old car. Or I can tell you that she drives a gorgeous, rare, red Bentley GTC. Both statements are true about the same car.

I can tell you that I authored *Million Dollar Consulting*. Or I can tell you that I've written more books on consulting than anyone in history. Both statements are true. I can tell you that I was chatting with Ted Turner once at a banquet in his honor. Or I can add that it was for a total of thirty seconds.

This is my problem with "humility." It's far too easy to be passed over, to be ignored, to be misunderstood. I played varsity basketball in high school. When teams chose sides for intramurals in college, I was odd man out, unpicked. Later, I mentioned to one of the captains my high school experience.

"Why the hell didn't you say something?" he asked.

Why, indeed?

Creating Personal Evangelists

Saul, who was to become Paul and later St. Paul, was virulently against the followers of Jesus. He beat them, hounded them,

---

* The Kardashians are not a new phenomenon. The Gabors—mother and three daughters—were doing the same thing easily in the much smaller world of the 1950s, and with primitive technology.

organized against them, and was on the road to Damascus to see if he could further instigate against them there.

On that road, it is said, he had his famous epiphany and became the greatest booster of what would become Christianity—and is easily its most prolific writer and evangelist. Paul was the first viral marketer, creating letters to and visiting scores of communities, from whence other evangelists went forward at Paul's behest.*

I use this example not for religious purposes but for emotional ones: there is a very thin line between love and hate—both are based on very strong emotions—and the epiphany need not be as dramatic as Paul's.

I found early on that having others speak on your behalf is far more powerful than speaking on your own behalf. Although I believe in "blowing your own horn" to stand apart from the herd, I also believe that a full orchestra is more impressive than a single horn, and you, personally, can only play one instrument at a time, in any case.

Hence, you need kindred spirits and soul mates who can attest to your character, ignite your cause, and generate major action. When I worked in large manufacturing plants as a consultant, I observed that union officials were very influential, but they in turn courted favor with highly respected workers. Employees who had been on the assembly line for twenty years, could do almost any job, and often helped train new employees were respected by management and labor alike. Workers like these were the people others looked to in support of their own agendas and goals.

When I worked with and managed large field sales forces, I found that there were salespeople who held no special hierarchical rank, but

---

* Historically, there are only shreds of evidence of Jesus's existence but tons of writing attributed to Paul and verified. We would know very little about the early church and about Jesus's life if not for Paul, who is far more important than even St. Peter, who has been acknowledged as the first pope.

whom others watched closely and listened to carefully. They might have shared sales techniques, or were ahead of their projections every year, or retained top clients with zero attrition. Whatever it was, they were respected and their views were sought and accepted.

You can see the same phenomenon among faculty members, athletes, politicians, attorneys, doctors, and financial experts. In almost every field, there are those who are influential not through hierarchical power or the power to reward and punish, but rather through the power of acumen, charisma, or track record. Call it "referent power," which I define as power derived from enormous and universally accepted credibility.

These are the people you want as your evangelists. Their endorsement, mention, and/or support do more than you could ever do through advertising or marketing or promotion. This is one reason that advertisers pay stratospheric fees for certain endorsements, believing that the quality of the product is almost insignificant compared with the quality of the endorser. Tiger Woods made tens of millions annually in endorsements because of his incredible success on the golf course, but all of those endorsements ended when he instead became associated with philandering.

There are people in my communities who tell people what they need to attend, how to use my services, and why they should invest now and not wait. They do this because they believe in me (their own success validates that belief), and they are effective because others believe in them as accomplished peers (their success is evident and manifest).

Mindsets: There is no one so zealous as the converted.

I mentioned Paul's change to begin this segment—and the thin line between the emotions of love and hate—because evangelists can emerge from unlikely places. Customers who feel mistreated but then find that the hotel or airline has taken dramatic steps to remedy their situation often metamorphose from rabid antagonists to diehard supporters. Companies and organizations are often rehabilitated in others' eyes through sincere apologies, rapid turnarounds, or changes in management, and former foes become hearty friends. My suggestions about evangelism and my lessons learned include:

• When you identify existing evangelists, treat them specially. Buy gifts or provide rewards or discounts when they have created positive situations and new business for you. Show them you appreciate every ounce of their support. Mention them publicly as valued clients and good examples.

• Give them the opportunity to evangelize. Mix them with your prospects. Hold joint meetings. Create forums where they can meet and social events where they can mingle. In my first Million Dollar Consulting® Convention in Atlanta in 2015, about 75 percent of the two hundred attendees knew me through my books and newsletters, but 25 percent—the evangelists—had participated in my high-end experiences, workshops, and coaching. The interactions between the two groups resulted in more than $150,000 in new business over two and a half days.

• Provide evangelists with something to talk about. No matter what business you're in, you can't coast. What new ideas, new intellectual property, new innovation can you continually expose people to so that they become excited in talking about you. Have you noticed that people such as Richard Branson and Elon Musk generate huge excitement around their endeavors, and there are people who back them and create buzz about them even if they have no particular stake in the undertaking? Their stake, rather, is in the charisma of the person and the person's ideas and creations.

Ask yourself a few questions:

- Who has served as an evangelist for you in the past?
- Who do you know now who is likely to serve as an evangelist?*
- What can you do to provide them with ideas and excitement around your goals?
- How can you arrange to intermingle them with those you most want to convert and influence?
- How will you recognize them for doing so?
- Can you reciprocate for them, making the bonds still stronger?

Evangelism works well in political contexts: the "occupy" movements, for example, and peace rallies. It works well in social contexts, such as the green movement and for causes such as abortion (on either side of the issue). But it can also work quite well locally: to improve the Little League field or set a Girl Scout cookie sales record, or to pave Main Street or improve street safety.

Paul was on the road to Damascus with fervor and deep feelings, which were reversed 180 degrees through his epiphany. What we need in order to create evangelists are those epiphanic moments, when people are convinced by others who so clearly believe in you.

Producing Your Own Reality

For most of my life I met people who told me why things couldn't be done. I was cautioned to play it safe, stay off the radar, keep my head down. The conservative and risk averse were to win the day,

---

* You can't accept just everyone. Politicians are continually embarrassed by support and financing offered by people with poor ethics, disturbed views, and offensive techniques.

which is like saying in a Darwinian world that it's better to be an eland than a lion.

When I worked at Prudential this conservative attitude was certainly evident. And this was true in most of the organizations I entered when I began consulting.

However, amidst the clarion call for caution—picture a lawyer as Paul Revere, shouting, "It could be that the British are coming, but it may well be that they're not, so don't do anything rash, pretend it's business as usual, and wait for more developments"—there were some people who clearly made me comfortable taking risk and creating opportunity. There were people who never panicked, who laughed at "bad news," who always found the road to their goal with an intuitive, inner global positioning system (which I'll discuss a little later).

I recognized what was going on. Despite the apparent reality around them, they created a new reality that better suited their needs. A couple of years ago in Walt Isaacson's terrific biography of Steve Jobs, he called this capacity "reality distortion." He meant that when rational engineers and designers gave Jobs a realistic time frame, he would cut it in half or by two-thirds and simply say, "Do it by that date." And, more often than not, they did.

Watch people in meetings or in conversations. There is a minority who will simply change the proposal, the projections, or the potential to match their own personal preferences and requirements. They dismiss precedent, question "facts," and blow through caution. We're accustomed to large amounts of time and money required to accomplish great things.

The original Hagia Sophia in Istanbul was constructed in five years (AD 532–37). The vast cathedral in Rouen required centuries; Hadrian's Wall took two decades. The "Big Dig" in Boston (a vast tunnels and road project through the city and to the airport) finished late and far over its budget. It's still experiencing problems from construction flaws.

Yet Olympic stadiums and venues are erected quite rapidly, Uber has taken over a major portion of city taxi traffic in just a couple of years, and we put a man on the moon within a decade using black box technology. In warfare, technological advances such as the revolving turret, submarine, machine gun, guided weaponry, and stealth capability were developed quite rapidly.

What we see is the urgency factor: when people want something badly enough they get it accomplished. They create their own reality in terms of what's possible and what can be done in the short term. But once you allow varied interests to be involved, or bureaucratic oversight, things slow down considerably, often to a crawl.

We can create our own reality. It is based on what we believe ourselves, what we tell others, how we tell them, and how we then behave.

Case Study

I was running my Million Dollar Consulting College® Graduate School at a Ritz-Carlton in Naples, Florida. I had asked senior management to address my group of twenty and give them some hotel issues to investigate while we were there.

The hotel manager began by asking the group, "How much experience do you have in the hospitality industry?" There was a 2-second silence, which to me was 1.5 seconds too long, so I said, "You're looking at twenty of the very best consultants in the world. Industry experience is not really a requirement given their consulting expertise."

"Of course, sorry," he said, and continued on.

After he departed, a participant said to me, "When you said these were twenty of the best consultants in the world, I looked around to see who you were referring to!"

I "created my own peers" by pointing out continually that Marshall Goldsmith (coaching), Seth Godin (creative marketing), Marcus Buckingham (self-improvement), Walt Mossberg (technology), David Maister (small business growth), and I (solo consulting) all owned our niches, and had very common traits (public appearances, books published, citations by others, and so forth). I hired Marshall and Walt and David to speak at my events. In short order, I found people in all kinds of traditional and electronic publishing citing several of us together at times to make their points. And one of the exercises I run today, when coaching entrepreneurs, teaches them to create their own peers.

That is how we can produce our own reality.

> **Mindsets:** If you allow others to create the ballpark, establish the rules, and hire the officials, you will lose that game.

The art of the setup demands that we take control of the creation of our reality. Are you a thought leader? Are you one of the top people in your field? Can you provide innovative ideas and implement them?

Think about the ridiculous quest for "humility." No one is shouting to get humble help. I don't want a humble automobile mechanic; I want one who believes he can solve any problem with the car quickly. I don't seek humble restaurateurs, but rather owners and chefs who feel (and claim) they can provide amazing experiences. Humility did not create Disneyland, nor send that man to the moon. Jimmy Carter tried to be a humble president, but that's not what's needed nor desired, and he wasn't successful in his quest for reelection.

Enthusiasm and confidence are essential to create your own reality. When you meet a prospect, the reality you should create is one of a peer meeting; don't go in as a supplicant or subordinate, even though the other person has a large office and huge title. When you go to a bank for a loan, it shouldn't be as a humble and meek homeowner in need of money, but as a potential partner of the bank. (If a bank loans you $100,000, you're a customer. If it lends you $1 million dollars, you're a partner.)

Case Study—Continued

When we embarked on the tough issues for the Ritz-Carlton, I told everyone how great it was to have this "live" opportunity and real laboratory in which to work and compare notes. We later presented our findings to management, who quickly went from skepticism to detailed note taking.

The same woman who questioned who the elite consultants were told me, "I thought this was going to be awful, didn't think we'd be able to help, and was afraid management would laugh at us. But you kept repeating how great it was, and how management would be blown away, and after a while I said to myself, 'Hey, this *is* pretty cool, and I think we'll crush this.' And that's what happened, because your enthusiasm was contagious."

I'm not bashful about telling people what to expect, what I will do, what they can do, and how things will look. I've told people who take two days to write an article that it should take them one hour, and they get it down to two hours. My "Book Proposal Sprint" began when a client asked if I could help him complete a book proposal in a year. I told him it should take a week but we'll take sixty days; thus far, dozens of people have done just that, and four, at this writing, have won publishing contracts while another dozen have agents.

We can create our own reality every day. All we need is the word.

CHAPTER 8

The Word

Many people scoff at language "purists" and insist that vernacular must prevail. Yet every business today is a communications business first and foremost, and the best of them craft very clear messages and establish tangible positions. There is no more powerful tool (or weapon) than words used with intent, purpose, and agility. Individuals and companies can rise above the "lowest common denominator" approach and dominate their markets. When I began speaking for money, I thought my common-sense approach would get me tossed out. What it got me was return engagements and high income.

Communicating at the Speed of Light

We're beginning to see rudimentary approaches to "retracting" those e-mails we've sent before we've been visited by common sense. I assume such software will be a hot seller. We've regretted leaving voice mail that we can't rescind. A lot of old physical comedy involved people trying to retrieve regretted letters from the postal delivery system (which was always astonishingly efficient in those programs).

Very early I observed that "trial and error," as a problem-solving approach, wasn't terribly inefficient *if the consequences of the error were slight*. You can correct a crossword puzzle, retwist a Rubik's Cube, try turning various circuit breakers on and off. In fact, this was often pretty fast. It didn't work so well when the consequences were severe (choosing a travel route) or dire (health decisions). Very few doctors have said, "The regimen here is trial and error: if this doesn't work, then try that, and if that doesn't work, try them together, then get back to me."

It also became apparent that you could easily test with a machine or process, as long as consequences were slight for poor decisions, but it was generally madness to use trial and error on people *because the consequences were always dire*!

It's one thing to test different makeup on your skin, try on a variety of clothing, or suggest some work regimens. But when you're not certain (and even if you are) it's generally unwise to say:

- You've lost weight.
- You've gained weight.
- You've changed your hair color.
- You've changed your hairstyle.
- You've changed your look.
- You seem calmer.
- You seem more energetic.

You get the idea.

In courtrooms, lawyers will deliberately say something that is improper, and the other side will object, and the judge will say the inevitable, "The jury will disregard...." Except the jury *can't* disregard, any more than you can unring a bell. The statement has been heard, the bell has tolled (for thee), the message is delivered.

Hence: the ability to communicate instantaneously—through e-mail, cell calls, texts, Instagram, Skype, and so forth—actually demands *that we slow down*. In those "days of yore" we wrote a letter, put it in an envelope, put a stamp on it, and placed it on a table to go out in the mail at a later time. We had the luxury of changing our mind and tearing up the letter, or writing one with somewhat less acidity and toxicity.

That's why I think e-mail software should have an option that allows you to choose that all e-mail is kept for an hour (or time frame of your choice) automatically before it is released. (This is possible on some software programs now.) We are communicating on thin ice these days, walking on the ice with a flamethrower, turned on, and pointed downward. No good can come of this.

So my first admonition about "The Word" is that you slow it down despite having the ability to make it faster than ever.

> **Mindsets:** Even in auctions, the first bid is seldom the winning bid, and in business the first suggestion is seldom the winning suggestion. The "firstest" also requires the "mostest."

We also talk too fast and use too much jargon. Words begin to lose their meanings. A strong "Thank you!" can be an expression of gratitude or sarcasm, or it can be an acknowledgment that you are supporting the other person. We tend to listen too fast as well. A school official in California was fired for racism after using the word "niggardly," until someone pointed out it meant "stingy" and he was (grudgingly) reinstated. There is a Rhode Island fast food joint in the casino at Twin River that's called Jeat, as in "Did you eat?" That was also how we spoke in New Jersey and New York (fuggedaboudit).

I coach people to take two beats (one thousand one, one thousand two) when they believe someone else has stopped speaking, before they respond. After all, the speaker may just be taking a breath.

I tell them not to "speak over" people, because volume doesn't carry a debate, though it may shut one down. (Deirdre Imus, wife of award-winning and controversial radio talk show host Don Imus, is the worst offender I've ever heard, simply yelling over others, and on some very controversial issues, such as her belief in the past that vaccination was a cause of autism, now scientifically disproved.)

When you're writing or texting, take an analogous two beats. You do this by rereading what you've written, twice. You may catch only typos and syntactical errors, but you may also catch the backlash of the over-the-top language you used.

Once a month or so, someone makes a routine request of me but with venom and hate. They might want to unsubscribe from a newsletter (which they opted to join) but ignore the instructions and fail to unsubscribe themselves. They blame this on me. Once I read the profanity, I take two beats—and leave them on the list.

Rapid communication works best with a succinct approach. People you are trying to reach are besieged with communications to the point that it's tough applying triage and finding the most important. I've found that people inevitably read what is brief. (Some publications, such as *Bottom Line*, specialize in a succession of very brief pieces.) I recommend that newsletters have four short articles (e.g., 250 words each), rather than one or two long ones.

In your e-mail signature file, one message is more likely to be read and remembered than five. In your promotions, one event is more likely to draw a response than a list of six. In your speaking, one idea is more likely to gain traction than four.

Many authorities cite "seven" as the most numbers in a sequence most people can remember most of the time. How many times have you been left a message with someone's phone number (typically ten digits in the U.S.) without a means to write it down, and you tried to remember it as you returned the call? I've done this and reached strangers in a variety of states and time zones. Your success rate is probably far less than that of a pelican diving for fish off the beach in rough weather.

Communicate with care, not haste, and with brevity, not verbosity. Give yourself the time to consider what you want to say *after* any emotional reaction has passed. The best response is seldom the fastest, it's usually the one that achieves your goal. I've stated repeatedly that speed *is important*, but don't be reckless.

You can try driving to your destination as fast as your car can go, but you'll be stopped by the police or you'll crash and perhaps not get there at all. Communications aren't very different, except there are no police. Be careful out there.

Persuading Through Metaphor and Example

Many years ago I was reading Margaret Wheatley's book *Leadership and the New Science.* I thought it an average book, sometimes almost impenetrable. (I've since met Ms. Wheatley and hired her as a guest speaker. She is highly cynical, to say the least, and her writing reflects a gloomy view.)

At one point, she made this observation in the book (paraphrasing): Consciousness is a function of processing information. Therefore, a dog is more conscious than, say, a clam, because a dog can process far more information.

I put the book down and had a revelation, an epiphanic moment. It's clear that some people process information at a far higher and faster pace than others; hence, they have a higher level of consciousness. This explained for me a chronic issue, where some people are rapid learners and some terribly slow, some are totally aware of their surroundings and some oblivious to them.

I thought of being in the presence of someone who was able to assimilate disparate parts of a complex event—a football game or a chess match—and one who seemed unaware of the unfortunate consequences of her actions—the person who pauses to look around at the bottom of an escalator, or pauses to discuss the completed performance in the middle of the exits. I began to create patterns and comparisons to better illustrate my thinking and instantiate it, removing the abstract and conjectural through the application of examples (such as those I just used).

My "oxygen mask" metaphor is based on the phrase we hear every time we fly: put your own oxygen mask on first before attempting to help others. The reason is that we can't help our family or other travelers if we, ourselves, can't breathe. That same principle applies to "healthy selfishness"—we can't help others unless we are comfortable. In other words, I can't provide pro bono help if I need to work every minute to feed my family. I'm far happier paying my kids' college tuition when I know that I'm not sacrificing a family vacation or a new car or going into serious debt to do so. I would do those things for my kids, but I'd prefer not to have to.

And, admit it, *we consciously or subconsciously resent those who deprive us of things important to us.* That's why the visiting relatives who usurp our time or impose on our privacy grow tedious very rapidly. That's why some of the most generous people I know are also among the most successful people I know.

Case Study

I was working with a hospital CEO who bemoaned the fact that his strategy wasn't being followed by even his direct reports.

"Where does it reside?" I asked.

He pointed to a shelf with a thick, three-ring binder. "It's all in there and every senior manager has one."

Realizing I was in a hospital, I said, "Bill, strategy is organic. It's a living thing that has to be tended daily, not thrust on a shelf to be seen by managers only on occasion and when forced to do so by the boss."

"Brilliant," he said. "Let's talk about ways to make that happen!"

We created protocols, which included senior people being evaluated on strategic goals met, every meeting starting with a review of the goals, all decisions of import needing to be consistent with the goals, and so on. It was a huge success.

A month later, a senior vice president approached me and said, "My colleagues and I want to offer you $10,000 if you can get Bill to *stop* using the term 'organic'!"

There are basically two ways to write a nonfiction book such as this one. The first is "scientific," which is what Malcolm Gladwell and Nassim Taleb and Dan Pink tend to do. They perform research, compare and contrast numbers and statistics, and present their findings, supported by facts such as the age that hockey players begin school in Canada or the numbers of hours an all-star athlete practices.

The second method is anecdotal. That is how Marshall Goldsmith and Seth Godin and I write. We support our points with examples to which the reader can readily relate. The oxygen mask phenomenon is one, and the person coming to a dead stop at the bottom of an escalator is another.

Both methods work, but the second is far faster. I remember Dan Pink, when he spoke at one of my events, telling me he needs months off by himself to organize and write his books. I can write a book entirely in two months. Dan is a better writer than I, but we both do well and many of my books are on the shelves for more than a decade (*Million Dollar Consulting* for twenty-five years and five editions, at this writing).

In business meetings and in attempts to influence others, my contention is that we need fewer statistics and more persuasion. I was introduced to one hundred financial executives as their keynote speaker, and every one of them had a digital device of some kind occupying some attention. I said, "You have those things forever, you have me for the next fifty-nine minutes, make a decision if you'd like to stay or leave before I begin." They all smiled and put the devices away, or at least did a great job keeping them out of my sight!

There is an urban myth that the aerodynamics of a bumblebee should prohibit flight but no one has told the bees. That's incorrect, but the point being made is fascinating (and an example of the anecdote being better than the science). People win, prevail, and triumph not because they are the scientifically best, but because they can bring the appropriate talent to the accurate place at precisely the right time.

Mindsets: We remember best and respond with most commitment to tangibles we can relate to in our daily lives, not abstract theory.

We identify with Thomas Edison talking about failure, and perspiration above innovation. Woody Allen observed that "eighty percent of success is just showing up."*

I have a great doctor, and I found him when a former doctor was driving me crazy with worry about minor symptoms he thought

---

* This is why we love the late Yogi Berra's oxymorons: "No one goes there anymore, it's too crowded." It's an example that contradicts itself. Allen quote: Wikiquote, https://en.wikiquote.org/wiki/Woody_Allen.

represented major illness, ordering a dozen tests. He wanted to keep using the science until he proved his theory, despite my discomfort and the cost.

My new doctor stunned me by saying immediately, "I doubt there's anything wrong, you don't look sick." And, indeed, he was right, simply using common sense.

What are you doing to persuade through examples (stories) and metaphor to make your point? What will people most readily relate to?

When I address an audience whose members are unfamiliar with me, I use that story describing how I was fired with poor severance and no savings, which prompted my current career. I ask if anyone in the group has ever been fired. This is a method of instant karma.

"It's a great club we're in, isn't it?" I ask, and then begin my remarks. That example provides an instant connection and camaraderie, far better than showing a slide with statistics about success factors and numbers of jobs held, believe me!

Translating and Reframing

Please remember these definitions:

Frame: A border enclosing something to be viewed.
Reframe: To change the border in your favor so that the viewer is seeing the issue in your context and perspective.

Masterpieces have beautiful frames, yet the viewer is nonetheless directed to the painting within the frame, not the frame itself. If you were to change the frame so that the portrait within it was seen differently, the Mona Lisa's eyes wouldn't be following you across the room and her smile wouldn't be nearly as beguiling.

The phrases "look at it this way" or "see it from my point of view" are actually requests that the other person use your frame, not hers. But your frame isn't easily applied, unless you make it manifest. (This is why the baseball strike zone—defined in the rules as a frame around the batter's midsection—is the subject of such controversy and argument. Each umpire has his own frame to which pitcher, catcher, and batter must adjust if they are to succeed. The pitcher can't say to the ump, "Hey, see that pitch from my view!")

As the editor-in-chief of my high school paper, I was invited to a competition in Philadelphia with hundreds of aspiring journalists. Our challenge was to write an editorial against drug use. My English teacher and newspaper advisor had driven four of us for three hours from northern Jersey, it was dreadfully hot, and I had a splitting headache.

Editorials, of course, are opinion pieces that usually represent the position of the newspaper on an issue, and are supposed to be written in the first person plural (using "we" and "our"). I couldn't wait to escape the room, so I wrote using the singular pronouns "I" and "my," and not as a newspaper representative but as a garbage collector who saw what was happening on the streets and who somehow had access to the newspaper for his piece.

I finished in twenty minutes of the allotted hour, and found a place in the fresh air and shade. A month later I was awarded first honorable mention—fourth place—out of the three hundred participants, and my advisor told me I had shown a lot of moxie breaking the rules.

But I hadn't broken the rules (or I would have been disqualified), I had simply changed the frame. And it was so refreshing, and so manifest, that the judges bought it. If I hadn't felt so lousy I probably would have won, but then again I probably wouldn't have been driven to the frame change.

This can work for you every day. Examples:

• A prospective buyer says to me: "We have never hired an external consultant in this operation, and have no plans to do so." I respond, "You have no idea how many of my best clients today began our first conversation with the exact same words." This changes the entire perspective from me as an outsider to him as an insider! I've completely reversed the momentum of the conversation.

• A prospect says, "We're on the West Coast, and you're on the East Coast." I respond, "That's exactly why you need me!" He has to listen to my next sentence rather than continue to try to show me why the distance is a deal buster. (We can use Skype, I'm on the West Coast monthly anyway, most of the work involves customers who are located around the country, and so forth.)

• A coaching client asked me what her next book should be about, because she needed help coming up with a premise. "That's the wrong question," I told her. "The real question is what you want your business to look like a year or so from now and what kind of book can drive people to that kind of business." Then we had a discussion that resulted in a book premise in twenty minutes.

Mindsets: Think of reframing as translating issues and discussions into your particular language of success. Most people don't even realize you're doing it.

To successfully reframe, you need to be clear on:

1. What is in *your* best interests to accomplish
2. What is acceptable to the other parties yet still in your best interests

3. How you can use language to reframe and translate the issue in a favorable and acceptable manner*

4. How to make manifest the new frame

In its ugliest forms, reframing becomes "spin," the primary weapon of political schlockmeisters. In its highest forms, it is statesmanship, diplomacy, and tact. But never lose focus that it's always to be used to promote your best interests.

The unappreciated problem you may well have is that *you're already often operating in someone else's frame*, and consequently you are meeting that person's objectives but not your own. This is sometimes done by accident or in the natural course of events (the truly enthusiastic with high volume make this happen), but it is sometimes done as I'm suggesting here—with careful thought and superb language skills.

Have you ever heard of "managing up" or "managing the boss"? This seems impossible until you consider it a version of reframing. You can do this with your spouse, partner, kids, and friends.

One day, on a lengthy conference call with clients, I wanted to get off the phone so I said, "I've been with you for forty-five minutes, the call is only ninety minutes, and you deserve to have some time to yourselves without my monopolizing it, so I'll check out now."

"Did you hear that?!" yelled one of my oldest coaching clients, "He just reframed his leaving as if it's in our best interests!"

Try to be less obvious than I was!

---

* For a detailed discussion of these techniques see my book *The Language of Success*, coauthored by Kim Wilkerson (New York: Business Expert Press, 2016).

Owning Transactions

I was the worst kind of Boy Scout. I couldn't swim well enough to be allowed to take out a canoe. I couldn't cook even if I had hauled my own barbecue to camp. I didn't know how to clean anything, though I had mastered the "how to get it dirty" part without much help.

One day in the mess hall at summer camp, I sat down with my tray and promptly spilled my milk all over my lunch of macaroni and cheese. Our scout leader briefly looked up, showed no emotion, and resumed his own lunch and reading.

It dawned on me that I was responsible for my own mess.

Later in the week I was drafted for cleanup duty after lunch, a loathsome job that denied me time to spend on activities I was not good at but that at least allowed me to relax. I didn't mind the others saying, "Weiss can't carve at all," as long as I gained the victory of not amputating a finger.

I found Vinnie, one of the senior Explorer Scouts whom I knew from my neighborhood a million miles from this forest of ineptitude. I told him that I was going to rendezvous with a girl from the camp across the lake (the ultimate and unargued reason to break any scouting rule) but I would miss my date if I were stuck here on KP duty. Vinnie promptly ordered me out ("I need this kid for the trail clearing at the lake"), winked, and wished me well on my tryst.

No more ruined lunch for me, I was going to run my own life (if it didn't require swimming, cooking, or carving).

Subsequently, I learned how to apply this system of not casting my fate to the wind but rather blowing back. I found that giving the right answers in class *makes the teacher look better*, because, clearly, people are learning. At Rutgers, my carpool partner was in only one class with me during four years—his major had something to do

with econometric analytics of financial subsets, so small wonder—
but he commented about that class, "I have never seen anyone be
a teacher's pet in college until now. It's amazing how she dotes
on you."

The professor was a tough-as-nails former army major who hated
poor discipline, with which she was surrounded at college. I was her
beacon.

In the world of consulting I found that one should *never, ever
allow the buyer to determine the consulting intervention.* We all
encounter the mouthwatering potential client where the buyer says,
"We need..."

a two-day strategic retreat
a leadership development program
a month of coaching
focus groups and surveys
a customer-focused culture
movement from good to great

The problem, of course, is that the buyer has arrived at an intervention and is simply seeking a contractor to fulfill the requirements.

Mindsets: A consultant is a brain, not a pair of hands. If you're
simply following someone else's direction, you're a hired hand. If
you're *providing* direction, you're a trusted advisor.

We need to own the transaction by using The Word. And The
Word is: Why? A one-word interrogative will carry the day. Because
"Why?" brings us to the real outcome and moves us away from the
arbitrary input. Example:

"We need a leadership development workshop."

"Why?"

"Because not everyone is making decisions consistent with our strategy at senior levels."

"Do you know why some are and some are not?"

"No."

"Well, why don't we find that out first, before jumping to a solution?"

Clients (and others) arrive at solutions first (before knowing cause or objectives) because of a great management and leadership myth, namely, that senior and important people are paid to take action. That is ridiculous.

Leaders are paid to get results.

Consequently, we have to establish what the results should be—the improved future state, the increased performance, the desired outcomes—before taking any action at all. Some of the best leaders I've ever seen manage only by exception. Some of the worst consistently try to demonstrate their importance through irrelevant actions. The baseball manager who takes out his strong, winning pitcher in the late innings because he believes that inserting a relief pitcher will demonstrate his management acumen—which is totally unneeded—often loses the game by imposing himself when imposition is a detriment.

A great many leaders are sucked into the vortex of moving from "good to great" without ever defining what "great" is for them, *or even investigating to see if they're already there!* That's the danger of a catchy phrase in place of smart management.

We have to own our transactions by not accepting the decisions (and often outright whims) of others merely because of their title, position, or budgets. The siren's call of "business at any cost" must be resisted.

Case Study

I was working at Mercedes-Benz North America, which at the time had a very rigid hierarchy within which people feared their bosses, right up to the president of the division, who reported to executives at Daimler-Benz in Germany.

As might be expected, the people who hired me (based on observing me elsewhere and meticulously investigating my credentials) began to tell me how to consult. They had a problem with uneven service at their dealers, and they demanded an analytic evaluation of service standards. I told them no, that's not what I would do; I'd go around to the best dealers and determine the best practices to spread down the line.

When they argued, I told them this: "Here's the deal. I won't tell you how to make brake pads or power steering units, and you don't tell me how to consult. You have auto experts falling from the rafters, but you need me because Lexus is eating your lunch because of their superior service."

That took care of it.

We don't lose control of our lives and fate, we cede it, surrender it, and leave it behind on the road. The simple act of owning your own transactions, taking accountability, and creating the ground rules will enable you to rule your world.

CHAPTER 9

The "App" of Success

The iPhone "app" intrigued me because it resembled a perpetual motion attraction machine (more phones, more apps, more apps, more phones, upsell apps, more buyers, and so on). I duplicated this approach in customer communities, with highly respected clients drawing more and more highly respected clients in a nonstop boom of marketing gravity and gravitas. Our real value is often most represented by the company we keep.

Attracting People Who Attract People

Some of you may remember this declaration from Lt. Col. Oliver North's lawyer: "Well, sir, I'm not a potted plant."* The implication is that we have innate value and are of no use if we simply sit passively. The entire idea in more contemporary society that students, for example, should be rewarded merely for attendance and not achievement is anathema to the world into which they will

---

* Famously uttered by counsel Brendan Sullivan defending Lt. Col. Oliver North during the Iran-Contra scandal in the late 1980s. Committee chair Senator Daniel Inouye had suggested that Sullivan allow North to speak for himself.

emerge—a capitalist, Darwinian system where manifested talent usually determines the winners.

We are not potted plants, nor do we want to surround ourselves with them once we leave our homes. The more apt metaphor these days is the "app."

Popularized by Apple more than any other source, the app is short for application of software to achieve specific ends, be they business, pleasure, financial, or simply diversion. My first iPhone had access to perhaps 250,000 apps, yet today, merely four phones later, there are millions and millions, a Carl Sagan universe of blinking, alluring apps.

Why so many? Because they draw so many customers. And they create an interesting dynamic:

- The more apps, the more potential uses
- The more potential uses, the more customers
- The more customers, the more appeal to future customers
- The more future customers, the more apps
- The more apps for the future, the more need for a new phone
- The more new phone technology, the more potential apps
- The more new apps, the more new customers

You can see a nice perpetual motion marketing machine here. What isn't so apparent is that this applies to us, in wholesale and retail (selling to corporations or individuals), and especially in professional services.

The old idea of trade and professional associations, with their monthly magazine and annual convention, is in its death throes. There is simply too little benefit and too high a cost. And the idea of "tribes," despite my great admiration for Seth Godin and his work, is the wrong emphasis. Tribes are exclusionary, rally around manda-

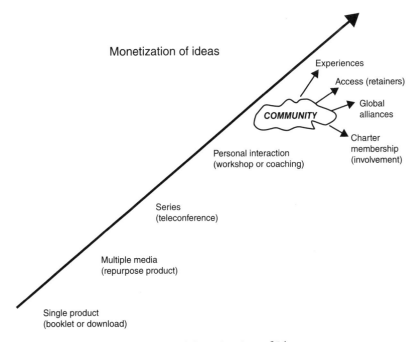

Figure 9.1: Monetization of Ideas

tory totems and rites, and seek homogeneity, with leaders chosen by ancestry or combat.

We are now in the age of community. A community is welcoming, heterogeneous, organized around talent and contribution, and focused on mutual learning and support.

Figure 9.1 depicts the evolution of a single product moving toward multiple media, in other words, a booklet that becomes a video or a workshop. It then morphs into a continuing series, perhaps a subscription service, using multimedia. For example, my Self-Worth ideas became a weekly video, audio, and print subscription globally. The next step is interactive—a workshop or coaching intervention.

However, our goal here is "community." The community

provides its members with experiences, events, connections, involvement, and continuing value *whether you are present or not.*

This is what I learned from apps! You can create a perpetual motion machine of value with frequent opportunities for people to invest in themselves, and either low-priced, high-volume offerings or high-priced limited offerings from you.

On AlansForums.com I've created the primary outlet for my global, 24–7 community. As I write this and as you are reading it, people are gathered there in real time or delayed time interacting with colleagues around the world, *and I am getting credit for those connections while I engage in other activities.* I'm on the Forum myself, accessible and contributing, several times a day, which I can do easily from any location that has an Internet connection (which today is like saying any place that has electricity).

No matter what field you are in or are considering, community has to be a logical and pragmatic goal. The days of the seller controlling information are long gone. Consumers now have access to all the information they need to make informed decisions, not only factual data but also opinions, reviews, and experiences of peers whom they trust. (Every survey you care to access will tell you that executive corporate buyers base decisions primarily on peer recommendations, not on sales literature and virtually never on social media sources.)

You form communities not by attracting one person at a time, but by the app principle: you attract people who attract people. You establish clearly that you are surrounded by people *whom others would truly love to cite as their peers.*

Mindsets: A community is a perpetual motion attraction machine. Focus on the exponential effect of every member drawing another dozen members. Keep adding new value—more "apps."

Communities involve meetings and events, access to private sites, subscriptions, coaching, and both formal and informal interactions among the members. That is, the interactions are instigated by the community "owner" *and* by the members. Some are free and casual, others are investments and organized. That's the essence of community—choice and options. There are no elites, no specially colored name tags or bizarre initials after names, just people who identify with one another, diverse but sharing common values.

Communities continue to grow, shedding some members (far fewer than trade associations and tribes), but sustaining growth because attractive, successful people are in abundance, drawing others constantly. There is really no barrier to entry.

Are you creating these opportunities with your clients, your buyers, your key recommenders?

The Power of Community

Not long after I was fired as the president of a consulting firm, and as I was searching for ways to promote myself as an independent consultant,* I received a call from someone at Merck whom I had worked with very early in my career with a firm in Princeton. He told me he had a project that they didn't want to award to a large firm. They needed a quick, agile approach with a very trusted source, and he thought I would be perfect.

"I'd love to help, Art," I nearly stammered, "but if I may ask, what made you think of me and how did you find me?"

"I asked for help from someone at your old firm," he explained,

---

* Ironically, the problem is seldom talent but rather simply creating the awareness that you exist!

"and she told me you would be perfect, that you had stayed in touch with her, and she had your contact information."

Mindsets: Evangelists are the most important promoters you will ever have, are free, and are nurtured by community.

I had begun an inadvertent community by informing all those among my contacts (pre-e-mail, pre-voice mail, pre-texting) about where I was (Rhode Island, of all places), what I was doing (organizational development consulting), and how they could help (send me leads). These weren't merely names collected via business cards while I "worked the room" at events. These were people who *knew* me and wanted to help, because I had helped many of them. I'm repeating the power of evangelism here because it grows quite rapidly in the hothouse of community.

When people hear of you from an independent source, they are far more inclined to believe in your quality than if you told them yourself! That's why endorsements are so important on book jackets and in advertising, and why the more recognizable the name, the more effective the evangelism. If I know you and respect you, I respect your recommendation. But even if I've merely heard of you and respect you, I'll still invest your recommendation with credibility.

Community is the greenhouse for such evangelism. It is a function of nurturing those who think highly of you and then presenting them with the opportunity to tell others. Our past clients (and friends, acquaintances, associates, and so forth) may love our work, but we can't assume that prospects and new people will necessarily feel the same way. After all, why should they? They have no evidence.

Evangelists are the means to transfer the high regard of those who know you to the knowledge base of those who do not.

Patricia Fripp is a colleague, one of the best speakers in the world, and my cohost for a decade at an event called The Odd Couple®. She would always tell a story about going to an event with a good friend, where they would split up and each would tell people about the other. Call it "orchestrated evangelism"! Fripp (she goes by her last name) would tell people she met while circulating amidst the crowd, "You'll never guess who's here, Susan Jones, the greatest coach in the country. If you like, I can introduce you. She's brilliant." Meanwhile, Susan was doing the same thing across the room for Fripp.

Politicians routinely use interest groups to represent their cause and election campaign. Religious leaders have used acolytes. Professional people have used interns. At one point, people involved in duels could have rabid followers represent them in the fight!

But I'm talking about those who *willingly, on their own initiative, and with great spirit* represent you and your talents and your position. That is the importance of community, where people are exposed to you and the others whom you have assembled (see the segment preceding) and believe in you and your work.

We can view this in figure 9.2, the Accelerant Curve.

The premise of the Accelerant Curve is that you attract people on the left with low barrier-to-entry offerings—free downloads, inexpensive booklets, newsletters, and so forth. (Adjust my examples for your type of business.) These are competitive, in that they are fairly common. Moving toward the middle, the offerings become distinct, cost more, and may take the form of audits, coaching, seminars, major events, and so on. Finally, on the right, we have breakthrough offerings that culminate in your "vault": value that only you can provide, such as special events, specialized coaching, retainers, licenses for intellectual property, and so forth.

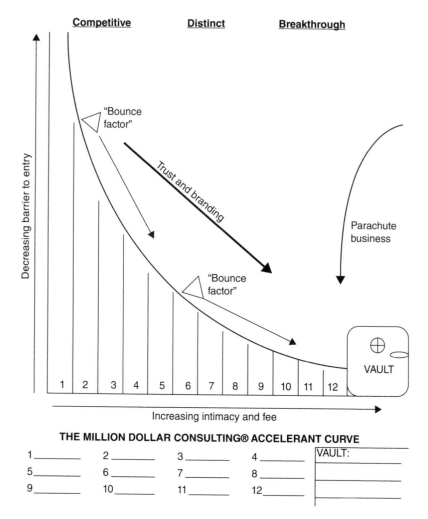

Figure 9.2: The Accelerant Curve

The "bounce" factors accelerate people still more. For example, someone reads my $25 or $35 book, such as this one, and then is motivated to attend my Million Dollar Consulting® College for $16,000. This happens regularly. Otherwise, trust and branding drive people down the accelerant curve, toward more expensive and less labor-intensive offerings.*

Evangelists both enlist people on the left side and help drive them toward the right side. They do this for free, because they believe in your value and *they experience it every day within your community.* That's why community is such a hothouse for creating support for your positions.

The Gravitas of Exceptionalism

President Obama has often been criticized by his opponents for abandoning the concept of American "exceptionalism." President Carter engendered the same reactions. The latter was criticized for his belief in the absence of grandeur—he wanted his motorcades to stop at red lights, and didn't believe in lavish state dinners or in manifesting the power of the presidency. The former has been accused of being too egalitarian with allies and offering apologies when critics believe none are needed to justify America acting in its own best interests.

The ability to attract attractive people (be they acolytes, evangelists, clients, prospects, media, or whomever) is based on appeal. That appeal is often called "charisma" (compelling charm and attractiveness), which is based on one's power, fascination, endeavors, success, and so forth. The iconic Steve Jobs had huge appeal for talented people, investors, and customers, but he was a mediocre husband and father, rather unhygienic, and often treated people

---

* That sounds counterintuitive, but it's not. People will pay more for intimacy but don't expect it all that often. See *Million Dollar Consulting* (McGraw-Hill, fifth edition, 2016) for a detailed discussion of value and fees.

around him poorly. Both Richard Branson and Elon Musk have become popular business heroes, luring huge investment despite some spectacular failures.

What is personal "exceptionalism" and why is it important to sustain our "app" of success? Is it merely charisma and popularity, or is it something else?

I was stopped in my tracks and fell down laughing years ago when I saw a cartoon in the *New Yorker* that showed two obviously wealthy men, in a posh men's club, talking over drinks. The one standing asked his colleague in a huge, comfortable chair, "You don't say, you owe all this to advice your father gave you? If I may ask, what was the advice?"

The other replied, "My father said, 'Here's ten million dollars. Don't lose it.'"

I fell down laughing because so many people I've met were born on third base and thought they'd hit a triple!

Exceptionalism isn't a birthright, nor is it based on a bank account. It is, however, the antithesis of the humility that so many people insist is the bedrock of success, when, empirically, nothing could be further from the truth. I'll repeat: I've never heard a client or prospect yell, "Get me a humble consultant!" or "For this key decision we need an advisor with great humility!" Leaders, powerful people, decision makers crave other strong people who are enthusiastic, excellent, and exciting. The want someone with a strong ego, not a huge sense of gratitude.

Over the years, Merck became my largest and most enduring client. Over twelve years of continuing relationships and perhaps thirty-five projects I garnered a substantial seven figures in direct work and another seven figures of referral work in other organizations. During this period Merck was named by *Fortune* in its annual poll "America's Most Admired Company" for an unprecedented five years in a row.

Two occurrences early on created my success track. The first was when a senior officer asked my advice on a new project and I gave him several options. He told me, "Alan, the reason we hired you is that we consider you an expert. We don't want to choose our option, we want your best option on how to proceed."

The second was when the president of the animal health group (who went on to be CEO of a rival company and proceeded to hire me again there) asked about a problem he was having, and I hesitantly explained that, as hard as it was to accept, his top lieutenant was the cause and had to be replaced. He calmly said, "Alan, we're both scientists (he had a PhD in chemistry) and I have no choice but to accept your conclusions." (I was tempted, shades of that program with the hotel management, to turn my head to see if an actual scientist with the same name had entered the room.)

Those two instances convinced me that I would never again put myself in a supplicant's position of tentatively suggesting solutions. I had to totally accept the *fact* that a great company had made the decision to hire me for my expertise, and that my appeal was the manifestation of that expertise in a confident, timely, and convincing manner. (Options given in order to be hired are one thing, options for proceeding *after* being hired are quite another.)

After these experiences, I began to tell prospects, "I'm the best possible person for this project, let's see how we can work together." Many were taken aback by that attitude, but they had no choice but to listen further and pursue the potential relationship.

Today, my communities—and their huge attraction of attractive people—are based on exceptionalism. There is no other learning and growth like it anywhere. I make myself accessible in a variety of ways and in real time. (Most of my colleagues, thought leaders in their own specialties and fields by wide acclaim, do not do this. Their communications are one way, top down, with no opportunity for dialogue or debate.)

I've never sought to be the "best." I've sought to be unique. Think of the Accelerant Curve from the previous segment. My offerings and "world" are largely vault items. You can become acquainted with me on the left and stick your toes in the water in the middle, but my communities are on the right.

> **Mindsets:** We are all unique. The key is to build a career around that uniqueness—what you are passionate about and great at doing—and carve away all else.

Early in life I had to choose between honest arrogance and hypocritical humility. I chose honest arrogance and have seen no occasion to change.

—Frank Lloyd Wright

In your life and your career, how do you "create" exceptionalism, and how do you sustain it without guilt, hubris, or false humility? Here are my guidelines for becoming exceptional, manifesting exceptionalism, and exploiting it for success. Remember the "oxygen mask principle": you can't help others until you've helped yourself.

• Your ultimate brand is your name. Attach your name to your accomplishments. I've received articles from people who neglect their own byline or fail to provide a biographical sketch. Don't write about "Ten Tips for Sales Success," write about "Dan Smith's Ten Tips for Sales Success."

• Protect your work. Use trademarks, copyrights, and patents as necessary to establish provenance and ownership.

• Stop trying to solve problems and start trying to innovate. "Fixing" things is a commodity endeavor, and most organizations are very good at it. But raising the bar is rare, especially for firms *already at the top of their markets.* Don't restore performance; create new performance.

- Share credit and be generous. Some of the most exceptional people I know are forever providing book endorsements, free publicity, and shared credit to others. It's a sign of magnanimity and confidence.*

- It's more important to know *why* you're good than *that* you're good. Assiduously explore the reasons for your success, not only so that you can replicate them, *but so that you can talk about them.*

- Never fear failure. If you're not failing, you're not trying. Admit defeat and move on. Exceptional people don't pursue blame and don't make excuses.

By definition, if you want to be exceptional you can't act like everyone else. Your GPS must have its own destinations.

Your Personal GPS

I was driving through North Carolina, having landed in Charlotte and needing to get to Raleigh. The rental car GPS was guiding me when I received a call from a coaching client. He had an idea he wanted to run by me that was so ridiculous, such a waste of time, and such a departure from the strategy we had agreed upon that I became incensed.

We argued for at least thirty minutes, and finally concluded the

---

* I gladly wrote a foreword for a colleague's new book, and "Foreword by Alan Weiss" went on the front cover, though I never requested it.

call with him agreeing to rethink the issue. As I looked around after hanging up, I thought I was on far too small a road. When I checked with the GPS, I found only a dark screen with a single arrow, seemingly lost itself. There were no landmarks, no roads, no directions. In my distraction, I had literally run out of GPS range.

We tend to do this with equal thoroughness in our lives and in our work. We become engrossed or distracted—or believe we can actually multitask effectively, which is a myth akin to unicorns—and "run out of known road."

I had a friend in college who told me during his divorce proceedings, "I was a happily married man until she told me she was leaving." I've worked with consultants fired during projects when they believed all was going quite well. One NCAA Final Four basketball game was decided when a star player called a time-out, though the team had no more; the team was penalized a technical foul, which the opponent made, and the other team won the game in the final seconds. The famous crashed Mars lander (at a cost of about $125 million) was the result of a California facility using centimeters and a Texas facility using inches—*and the memo that discovered the lack of coordination by an engineer was misplaced and ignored.**

GPS is supposed to keep vehicles on track to their destination, but GPS is worthless if it's not turned on, is ignored, or is not working properly. What constitutes your personal GPS? What kind of guidance systems do you need to reach your destinations? This is part of the app for your success.

I believe that these are your requirements:

1. The software has to be in place. That means that you have the information about your current position, environment, routes,

---

* http://www.cnn.com/TECH/space/9909/30/mars.metric

and destination in mind. There is no "uncharted territory." In practical terms, you need:

- An ongoing strategy that describes what your business and lifestyle should look like in the near future, a moving vision of where you want to go.
- The ability to recognize success—the "why" of success, as we discussed earlier—and to replicate it. These are "routes" that you want to maintain in memory.
- The recognition of your current starting point, which changes. Are you growing? Do you have new needs? This will help determine if memorized routes are still useful or not.

2. Availability of the system in good working order. You'll require frequent if not constant use of your system. Don't attempt to use trial and error or "gut feel." Every successful person I've ever met has a process for success. Sometimes people can't (or won't) articulate it (and I have to help them to do so), but they are never successful by random flips of a coin.

- Use quick and pragmatic aids. You don't want to lug a laptop into a prospect's office or use extensive notes when trying to convince people in a discussion. Use visuals that people can focus on, and keep a few bullet points in front of you. PowerPoint presentations are soporific, not stimulating.
- Work backward from successfully reaching your destination (new job, award, new customer, better relationship) and ask yourself exactly how you achieved it. It is never about luck. The harder your work, the luckier you get.

3. You must update for changed conditions. "What got you here won't get you there," observes coaching guru Marshall Goldsmith. As you progress through various stages of growth (which I'll

discuss in the next chapter) you often change your starting points, destinations, routes—even your vehicles.

- Many people get "stuck" because they don't abandon their original starting point: the old friends, the old habits, the old expectations. Growth requires that these change.
- A high-performance car can travel faster and more safely on superhighways than a clunker. An SUV can carry more people. What are you driving now?
- This is a journey, not a trip. Destinations must keep changing or you'll be stuck in a dead end.

Mindsets: Only the gifted few can wing it. "Playing by ear" never results in truly great music, and the "seat of your pants" is usually busy bearing weight.

As a maverick, your personal navigation is critical because you're going to abjure the usual paths and recommended lanes. In Nantucket, where I'm writing this, you can travel up quaint but torturous cobblestone streets—which must have given horses fits a hundred years ago—to get from downtown to our beach house in Madaket. That's the route that the realtors will tell you to take, and the one most GPS systems advise.

But we found a back route that is completely paved. It goes through small streets and myriad turns and you often have to pull over to allow someone to pass in the opposite direction, but it's a fun drive and far more comfortable. We found our own way, and we don't tell anyone about it except our family (and I was hesitant about that).

My own GPS told me that moving up the corporate ladder, despite all the security and vacations and retirement packages, was not the route to my goals. A lot of people made poor choices, using traditional directions, when massive layoffs, pay cuts, and benefit reductions undermined those routes. I knew when I was fired that my new GPS was guiding me to never work for anyone ever again. This guidance system enabled me to comfortably turn down a variety of job offers as I was forging my independent career. Too many people are simply chasing money with no guidance at all. They will sooner or later drive into a wall or over a cliff.

I incorporated into my guidance that respect was a more important destination in my work than affection, and adapted an appropriate persona toward clients. My routes were always guided by the "oxygen mask": I had to have a route that was positive for me if I was to help others. I would not let others drive me in uncomfortable ways toward undesirable ends.

What are your routes and destinations? Are they installed in your personal GPS? In our final chapter, allow me to help you accomplish that on your personal journey.

CHAPTER 10

No Guilt, No Fear, No Peer

Remember, There Is Always a Bigger Boat (TIAABB). The point is to find comfort in one's own skin while moving from a poverty mentality toward an abundance mentality (as has been the flow of this book). To achieve this, we must consciously change relationships, beliefs, interests, and even values—and seal the "watertight doors" behind us so we don't revert. (Have you seen successful people who never reach for the check or become paralyzed when faced with a needed purchase?) We need a mantra of "life, contribution, and success."

The Four Levels of Existence

A few years ago we were in St. Bart's and I strolled along the harbor while my wife shopped. It's a deep-water harbor, and there were a dozen huge yachts taking up every mooring that could accommodate such behemoths. There were another two dozen anchored in the bay, either because there was no room or because the beasts were too big to fit in even these huge berths. (I've never known what the ego issues were when you had the biggest boat but no one could see it!)

The boats, individually impressive, I'd guess, were rather boring, lined up in a sort of parking lot, all huge, all with assorted accoutrement; one became accustomed to their presence and forgot about them.* The fact that one yacht was larger than another didn't matter at that size. (It's been said that Paul Allen, cofounder of Microsoft, and the Sultan of Brunei would build extensions on their boats so each could claim "mine is bigger than yours.") The Russian billionaire Andrey Melnichenko, had a $300 million yacht moored in Monaco the last time I was there, deliberately designed (by Philippe Starck) to look like a hybrid of a submarine and the battleship *Potemkin*.

I learned long ago, there is *always* a bigger boat.

It's senseless to pursue the biggest and "most" of material things. It makes all kinds of sense to pursue those material (and aesthetic) goals that bring meaning to your life and support your lifestyle. Simply looking for "biggest" (as a metaphor) always means you're pursuing someone else's metrics and standards. Mr. Allen and the sultan certainly must have a great deal of time and money on their hands to pursue largest boat status, but to what end? Bill Gates and Warren Buffet, as two examples, seem to prefer giving money to charities and pursuing philanthropic goals. They don't try to give the "most" or more than the other, they just give.

One of my most important lessons in life has been that I have to pursue what's right for me, not what's right for someone else.

I've identified four levels of existence on the success path. You can see them in figure 10.1.

1. Survive: This is the equivalent to the basic level on Abraham Maslow's famous hierarchy of needs, though we're looking at

---

* Compare this to the observation of Eleanor Robson Belmont, stage actress and later wife of a billionaire: "A private railroad car is not an acquired taste. One takes to it immediately."

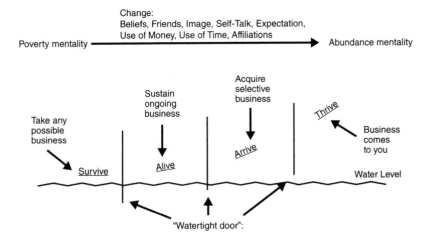

Figure 10.1: The Watertight Doors

survival in terms of career and family. A person in survival mode is trying to feed the family and pay the bills. I recall distinctly when my parents used to argue about how to beg, borrow, or connive the $40 monthly rent payment, usually when it was already overdue.

People in this position will take almost any kind of business, will scrimp and save, will not invest in themselves, and exist with a poverty mentality—they don't spend anything not absolutely essential to survival. Many of us are there when we begin an independent business without adequate preparation, such as when we've been fired!

2. Alive: This level is reached when we know we can sustain a basic lifestyle and can begin to save a bit, pay down debt, and plan a future beyond tomorrow. Our business is stable if not rapidly growing, and we're able to successfully bring on new clients and maintain current ones. We have far less angst about day-to-day existence.

This is the time that extended family members may stop ranting that we never should have launched our current endeavor.

3. Arrive: Here we have sustainable growth. We are saving and investing. We reap the dividends from investing in ourselves. We can take (sometimes uneasy) vacations. The work we take on is more selective and we don't just accept work because there is money attached. People begin to seek us out.

When you "arrive" you have reached stable growth and a comfortable lifestyle.

4. Thrive*: This is when you are an object of interest, a thought leader, the person others seek out. People come to you. You design your life; it's the difference between purchasing a fine suit (arrive) and a bespoke suit. Your name and brand impress others and you are known.

Mindsets: You can always make another dollar, but you can never make another minute.

You make intelligent decisions about lifestyle and career without guilt or concern about the metrics of others. You take prudent risk. You allow yourself the freedom to fail. By anyone's measure you are a success, *not by what you own but by who you are.* Most importantly, you are a success by your own measure.

The huge problem with these four levels—and I've created them in this manner for clarity and to make distinctions—is that people who attain various levels of progress don't always act this way. There is often a huge cognitive dissonance between who people are and how they act. We're used to the poseur who pretends to be more than he is, but we're much more likely to encounter people who cannot accept their success and who never enjoy their status.

---

* For the record, my book *Thrive* was written years before Arianna Huffington's.

The person with money who looks at a dinner check as if it's a coiled cobra, the successful professional who is concerned that she has been lucky and next year will be a disaster: these are the people whose perspectives do not grow with their successes.

How to Seal the Watertight Doors

As we move through these stages we need to emerge on the new level. We can't go slip-sliding back and forth. Picture the doors on a ship: they have wheels and battens to make them watertight. The *Titanic* sank because its "watertight" compartments weren't. The water was able to overlap them because they weren't completely sealed.

You don't want to hit a personal or career iceberg and, if you should, you don't want it to sink you.

It's a natural progression from "survive" toward "thrive," but many people can't maintain their new level because they never sealed the doors behind them, and they keep sliding backward. This isn't an abstract principle. You've seen it in situations like this:

• A wealthy person keeps his hands behind his back during spirited bidding at an auction. He winds up winning a bid for $150 in the silent auction when the live auction raised nearly $100,000.

• Someone stares at a check after dinner as though it were anthrax-laden.

• Highly successful people—who talk easily about their success—are selling old luggage on eBay or buying secondhand clothes.

• A person is always asking for a deal, despite the inappropriate nature of the circumstances, for example with a local merchant or a charity.

• If someone else is paying for a dinner or event, a guest asks for the most food, the most expensive drinks, and tries to bring a family member along.

Case Study

A guy in my community was a self-proclaimed elite, but we all knew the expensive cars belonged to his father-in-law. He was always trying to get a deal, always claiming that he was better than others.

During an expensive event I was hosting, he asked, inappropriately, if he could take his wife to the group lunch. I agreed, though no one else even considered doing so. At lunch, both he and his wife ordered the lobster special—a $50 entrée.

Neither ever said thank you.

Sealing the watertight doors is difficult. That's because we have to make changes to seal them. We probably have to make changes in:

• Habits
• Memberships
• Friends
• Beliefs
• Behaviors
• Values
• Use of money

I met a man, a former naval officer, who told me he wanted me to coach him, but in consideration of the normal fee I had to "throw in" a few of my books for free.

"Why would I do that?" I asked.

"Because," he proudly claimed, "for the last ten years I've always received something for free or a discount on every deal I've made, so I want to continue the streak."

It was an absurd request in an inappropriate dynamic. But he couldn't give it up. He couldn't batten that hatch.

Do you find yourself debating whether to do something when *the alternatives really don't matter*?! Today a woman who makes $650,000 a year asked if it was worth upgrading from an American Express Gold Card to a Platinum Card. Some people were giving her particulars about the differences.

"Why are you even asking?" I asked. "Perhaps this was a quandary for you ten years ago, but what difference does it make today? Get the Platinum Card."

> **Mindsets:** If you find yourself debating things that are irrelevant in your current situation and success, you're sliding back through open doors to previous levels.

When we're at "survive" and "alive" every penny may count. Personal sacrifice may be called for on a regular basis. We may have to practice thrift and conservatism. However, at "arrive" and "thrive" we are controlling our destiny, we have reserves, and we know we can make more money. It's silly to spend $500 worrying about how to save $10—yet that's exactly what people do when they drive five miles out of their way to save five cents a gallon on gas for the car.

Case Study

There are only two of us who have ever been named to both the Speakers Hall of Fame® and as fellows of the Institute of Management Consultants.

When I spoke for a local chapter of the IMC in the Midwest, they needed to procure a wireless lapel microphone for my talk. The other person with my honorifics, who belonged to the chapter, brought his personal microphone for my use. I told the chapter president that the gesture was very kind.

"Not really," he said, with a wry smile, "he demanded that in return we waive his $49 meeting fee!"

The failure of people to move forward is based largely on their adhering to the past, no matter how illogical. In fact, that inability to let go is highly emotional. "Can I get the early discount even though I missed the deadline?" asked someone who was making a million dollars a year. "You know I can't do that, and the $150 difference means nothing for you, so why do you even ask?"

"I have to ask," he confessed. "I always need to try to get a deal."

For many, their upbringing and parents cause this phenomenon. It's been ingrained in them to preserve, to deny themselves, to save. For others, it's their partners and spouses who have become "underminers" by questioning whether current success can ever be replicated and suggesting that luck had far more of a role than talent in their current status. And for others it's abject fear: of being "found out" as an imposter, of having stumbled upon good fortune instead of having created it, and of losing the competitive race to others who exhibit more confidence and tenacity.

We seal the watertight doors and eliminate guilt and fear by consistent and deliberate change, upgrading our own image, surrounding ourselves with appropriately supportive people, and improving our self-talk. We need to practice positive psychology with ourselves so we can redirect our emotions to thrive, and so we can seal the doors behind us.

That calls for moving permanently from a poverty mentality to one of abundance.

Moving from a Poverty to an Abundance Mentality

Welcome to the most important aspect of this book for many of you. It's relatively easy to spot a poverty mentality and to appreciate the hallmarks of an abundance mentality. But how do you make the transition?

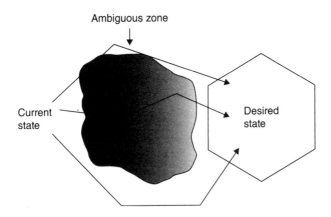

Figure 10.2: The Ambiguous Zone

Remember my visual about the ambiguous zone? You can see it again in figure 10.2. This is the essence of traveling from a poverty mindset to an abundance mindset, *because that road varies for each of us.* We know what the desired state is, and we know where we are, but the transition is often murky and frightening.

I chided my son once when we were at the amusements on the boardwalk at Wildwood, New Jersey, when he resisted going into the funhouse. "Don't be afraid of the dark," I admonished him.

"I'm not afraid of the dark," he assured me, "I'm afraid of what might be in the dark!"

I had no comeback for that quite logical reasoning. After all, the absence of proof isn't proof of absence. There just might be a monster under the bed that you've never been able to see. There are people who believe in spirits, in UFOs, in true magic. Religions are based on faith and belief, not evidence, yet billions of people have been guided by those tenets.

So the question becomes, "How do we transit the ambiguous zone from poverty to abundance without being scared by what we might encounter?" And the answer is: we need to throw some light on the issue.

What we are likely to encounter are fears, pure and simple. In fact, we should expect to bump into them and recognize that they must be confronted rather than enabled, destroyed rather than empowered.

> **Mindsets:** We are often shocked into immobility by abject fears without basis or rationale. Hence, we can't eliminate them and they self-perpetuate. We need to find the *cause* of our fears.

When we fear, our talents are masked, and this is not unlike being depressed or being burdened with guilt. We do not operate at our optimum capacity and are, therefore, even less able to combat the fears. We can see this (or have experienced it ourselves) with speakers who are so nervous that their mouth dries up and their voice is strained. They were afraid of people not reacting well to their talk, and now *they've created the exact dynamics to make the audience unhappy with their talk.* We see it in athletes who choke under pressure, nervous about not performing well to the extent that they don't perform well.

There is a difference between choking and panic, by the way, useful to understand when attempting to traverse the ambiguous zone. When you choke you know what to do but can't do it well because of your fears of not performing well. So the golfer misses an easy putt and the salesperson makes a lousy presentation because they are so worried about others' reactions, their own self-worth, and the stakes represented by success or failure.

When we panic we forget entirely what we have to do. The golfer doesn't generally forget that there is a need to hit the ball with a club and put it in the hole. The salesperson understands that the people in the room must be convinced of the value of an offering. But the scuba diver whose regulator stops working at forty feet and panics is unable to remember the simple procedure of reaching over his shoulder to obtain the backup regulator. That person will die.

Consequently, to move from poverty to abundance—to traverse that ambiguous zone—we need "light" and calm, and to confront our fears. We need guidance, that GPS I spoke of earlier. Here is my guidance system:

- Recognize the behaviors you wish to exhibit. Stop worrying about what you want to *end* and focus on what you want to *begin*. For example:
  - I will pick up the check without hesitation in a group.
  - I'll use short-term debt to finance a vacation.
  - I'll consider making those impulse purchases.
  - I will resist inappropriate client requests.

- Ask yourself what is stopping you from achieving the new behavior and note the reasons:
  - I fear monthly credit card debt.
  - My parents would have called me irresponsible.

- ○ I'd feel guilty the next day.
- ○ It's horrible to lose any client.

- Apply a rationality test to the fears:
  - ○ I can easily pay credit card debt monthly up to this amount: $XXX.
  - ○ My parents lived a conservative life with little joy and were skeptical about my current career, which is a huge success. They loved me, but they weren't always right.
  - ○ I should ask my partner or spouse about the purchase to make sure it's appropriate (unless it's a gift for my partner, in which case I would never feel guilty).
  - ○ I've brought new clients on repeatedly, and I've lost them from time to time, but my business continues to grow. And poor clients rob my time from good clients.

- Finally, decide how you'll support and bolster the new behaviors:
  - ○ I will give the server or manager my credit card before the meal or drinks so I don't have to make a show of picking up the tab.
  - ○ I need to set the model for my own children and family, and not convey the one that had undermined me, so I'm going to exhibit more innovative and progressive attitudes.
  - ○ I'm going to reaffirm the next morning how happy I am with what I've purchased, and also watch how happy my partner is with the purchase.
  - ○ I will establish criteria for clients, such as paying on time, not making unreasonable requests, providing me with learning, and always acting ethically and honestly. My criteria will determine who stays and who I allow to go.

The list above offers examples of how to shed some light in the ambiguous zone. Your examples will differ, but you can confront them in the same manner, with same sequence.

What are you afraid of in the dark?

Is it really there?

If not, end the fear.

If so, create new, more rewarding behaviors and reinforce them.

As I've mentioned, it's important to have a partner or spouse and friends and colleagues who support these growth goals and don't undermine them, who believe in abundance and not poverty.

But the fundamental issue is *your* personal philosophy, beliefs, and values. Those constitute what is a very personal journey.

Your Personal Journey

This chapter is titled "No Guilt, No Fear, No Peer." It sounds arrogant to some. No matter. It's the elixir for your personal success, as it has been for mine.

I have found people plagued by guilt. The guilt is often imposed by parents (living or, worse, deceased). It is often imposed by those around them. And, insidiously, it is frequently self-imposed. Guilt is a feeling of having done something wrong, or the belief that you may do something wrong at any given time if you're not extremely careful. The default position should be innocence, but in the psychological court of law, many people are guilty until proved innocent, and they have no defense attorney.

I mentioned to a clinician friend of mine, a therapist with a PhD, that I had overcome feelings of guilt and felt "guilt free." She unhelpfully pointed out that this was also one of the traits of a psychopath!

But, you see, that's the issue: we've become imbued with the sense that we somehow *should* feel guilty and that it's unnatural not to. The mental disorder is having no guilt! At first it sounds humorous, but when you delve deeper, it's stopping people in their tracks. More than any religious belief about sinners and salvation, societal and psychological guilt is eroding the borders of our happiness and delimiting the potential of our talent.

Case Study

For many years, four of us—all top consultants—worked with the CEO of a major insurance company. He was successful in his work, having been recruited from senior vice president of one firm to become CEO of another. Yet he was married to his third wife, many years his junior, and they eventually were embroiled in a nasty divorce. He was depressed to the point that he required medication. He was in therapy frequently.

The underlying issue was that his father, still alive, had told him constantly that he would never amount to anything, and the father continued to tell his son that, dismissing his son's current responsibilities as minor and unimportant. Our client was unable to shake that, and was eventually fired when he didn't pay close attention to a subordinate's decision, which cost the company a small fortune.

He constantly felt guilty about not having been successful enough, not having pleased his father, not having lived up to ridiculous and irrational expectations.

He is still working out the financial damages from the third divorce.

We all know a great many people who feel guilty nearly all the time. I've seen guilt all around me as I grew and prospered:

- I can't buy this, who am I to spend so much money?
- I can't justify this since I'm not paying full bonuses to my employees this year.
- I don't deserve this, I could have done much more.
- I need to give more to my family despite their ill will; I've been lucky and they haven't.
- We can't take a vacation and leave the kids with our parents, it's unfair.

Until the sixteenth century, almost everyone truly believed there was an afterlife and would do anything to ensure entry into heaven: pay for indulgences, tolerate corrupt clergy, deny themselves basic needs.

Is it really any different today?

This is how you can free yourself of the daily, subconscious, automatic, default mechanism of guilt:

1. Embrace the concept of "earning." I earned this because I worked for it, because of my talent, because of my risk taking. This was not money or a promotion or an opportunity that was created by luck or unfair practices. I competed and won.

2. Life is not a zero-sum game. Your "winning" does not mean someone else must "lose." Your success does not remove opportunity or success from others. You are not engaged in a hydraulic system where someone has to go down for you to go up.

3. Ignore those who attempt to instill guilt. Your religious life should be about tolerance and forgiveness. Your social life should revolve around positive, optimistic people. Your married life should be about mutual support and growth. And your extended family should be involved with joy and respect. *You need to adjust or depart from any of these that produce ongoing guilt.*

You can see family less, change churches, find new friends. You can't afford to be married to someone (or be in a long-term intimate relationship with someone) who constantly generates guilt. If you don't make these strong decisions, you will be ground down to insignificance. ("How can you make that trip and leave me here alone with the kids?" "Sure, buy things for yourself while the rest of us are trying to be frugal." "Why don't you support your brother, it's not his fault he got mixed up with the wrong crowd." "You are nothing but a disappointment.")

4. Recognize success and avoid feeling that you are not "successful enough." Those around you can inadvertently (and, toxically, advertently) undermine your efforts and enflame guilt by pointing out: "You were first in your class, but your grade point average was less than your sister's when she was first." "You were recognized for your work, but it's a small company in a small town."

5. This all results in this admonition: *Never rely on others for validation.* You must create and maintain self-validation. You have to know who you are and what truly constitutes success in business and in life. Speakers who live or die based on ratings sheets and standing ovations are pathetic. They desperately need others to validate them (a common theme on Facebook: please "like" me). You can't allow *anyone*, whether family or friend, to determine your validity and success.

Mindsets: If you rely on external validation to tell you whether you are worthwhile and successful, you will be neither in any meaningful way. These are your decisions. Don't abdicate them.

Fear is about discerning what you should really be afraid of: someone with a gun, a tornado, a poisonous snake. I've never met any of these in a buyer's office, at a restaurant, in an audience, or at a conference.

My father volunteered for the first U.S. parachute regiment ever formed, some time around 1940. They originally jumped from cargo planes with no reserve chute from about five hundred feet. After Pearl Harbor, his unit fought to defend Australia, and they jumped at Lae, New Guinea, into Japanese guns in the jungles. A large part of his unit was lost.

I asked him why he did that. He told me he thought it was a good idea at the time.

At this writing, he is ninety-nine and living independently.

No one is shooting at you. There is no giant lever next to a buyer that triggers a trapdoor to dismiss you, as there were in old silent movies and cartoons. You can't leave a buyer's office with less than you walked in with. Even a rejection should result in learning.

No one is shooting at you when you make a speech, dine with friends, take a test, or even argue with colleagues. There is no snake, no tornado. We spend far too much time being afraid of nothing at all. I've been in five planes struck by lightning over the last thirty years. And here I sit.

My dogs don't enter the yard each morning with trepidation or decked out in survival gear. They go tearing out to explore. They do the same in unfamiliar surroundings. They rely on their senses and their wits. The last time I looked, we were a tad higher on the evolutionary scale than canines.

Fear (like guilt and resembling depression) will mask your talents, undermine your efforts, attenuate your effectiveness. When we're fearful we hesitate, vacillate, sometimes hide. Fear can be paralyzing physically, which is why people stumble as if clubbed when they have to speak or present something in public. It's why hands shake on putters and people draw blanks (panic) on tests.

We need to rationalize fear so that it's in its proper compartment:

1. Perform triage. Is what I'm concerned about truly going to end my career, or possibly result in an error, or perhaps embarrass me if I'm wrong? Or will no one care at all?

2. Always ask, "What is the worst that can *reasonably* happen?" On a cruise, the ship isn't going to sink, although you might get seasick, so take proper precautions. In a speech, the audience isn't going to boo, though they may get bored, so use some visuals and group interaction. When you are meeting new people, they aren't going to interrogate you, though they may have trouble making conversation, so practice some discussion points and questions.

3. Stop fearing the unknown. We live on a hunk of rock traveling at about eighty thousand miles per hour around an exploding star. We have no idea of the limits of the cosmos or even what is in the center of our own planet. You may be in the ambiguous zone, but you can shed light, not fear it. Explore, don't flee. Remember the admonition (I believe from St. Augustine) "There are no miracles, only unknown laws."

4. "Fight or flight" is a primitive psychological reaction to perceived threat. We become combative or we run away. That's fine for the Serengeti, but not Main Street. I'd suggest an intermediate position: "right." What's the right thing to do? It's seldom fight or flight. It's usually something far more prosaic, such as problem solving, or decision making, or priority setting. Don't allow perceived fear to force you into arbitrary reactions. Think about what's right.

5. There are irrational fears that require help. Fear of heights or public speaking or crowded places requires therapy if you are to overcome it. Some fears are deep and encrusted, and require a professional to expose and help remove them. There is nothing embarrassing or weak about seeking that kind of help. In fact, it's a great sign of strength to do so.

Once we've understood the need to conquer guilt and fear, we're left with the pragmatics of dealing with the world around us. I've taken a maverick stance for quite some time on this issue. You may find it untenable or even unacceptable, but I suggest that, if you've read this far, you keep reading.

"No peer" means that I deliberately do *not* see myself as an equal member of a group. While I take a position as a peer of the buyer whom I'd like as a client, or of someone else's spouse to whom I'm introduced at dinner, I don't really feel that way. I feel I'm the smartest guy in the room *until proved otherwise.*

I don't stand on stage (or write this book or coach others) with the idea that we're all colleagues and I'm fortunate to be in a position to share. That kind of pseudo-humility is corrosive and unimpressive. I take the position that, in my fields, I'm the expert. I know more than you. And acknowledging that (no guilt) without any expectation of resistance (no fear) *makes me even more effective in helping you.*

I want a world-class lawyer, chef, surgeon, CPA, even designer or landscape architect. I might ask them questions, but I'd never consider myself a peer in their business or profession.

I don't allow clients to tell me how to consult or coach. "We need you to facilitate a three-day strategy retreat," I'm sometimes told. "And why is that?" I ask, instead of citing them a fee for three days and patting myself on the back. The result has often been a six-figure project that has nothing to do with a strategy retreat. I know how to consult and improve the client's condition, otherwise, why even talk to me?

The difference, however, is that when we're *not* talking about our respective specialties, I feel I have no peer in the room. I am well educated, well traveled, have raised a wonderful family in a long-term marriage, have created a hugely successful career, have written sixty books—no, I think I have more to offer on "neutral ground" than anyone else present *unless it's proved otherwise.*

You don't have to have my credentials; you'll find your own are very impressive *if* you have no guilt and no fear. The ability to operate and live with confidence and conviction (ability and passion) alone will carry the day almost all the time, because others are burdened with so much superfluous baggage. You have to be aware of your own story and your own strengths. (Remember the example earlier of the woman with "no story" who had gone to West Point?)

If you are willing to accept the complete sense, and the benefits, of a "no peer" philosophy, here's some help:

1. Don't be easily impressed by attempts to impress you. When I'm introduced to a doctor socially, I use his or her first name, as he or she would use mine. The honorific is unnecessary in that setting. Titles are often deceiving (everyone in a bank is a vice president, including the janitor—vice president of post-operating hours sanitation). I know a great many college professors who don't know which silverware to use and whose grammar is problematic, no matter their expertise in Ecuadorian topography or petri dish sterilization.

2. Never try to compete for the sake of competing. One-upsmanship is a personality disorder in my book. If someone

comments that she is just back from the Excelsior in Venice, don't reply that you've stayed at the far superior Danieli. Simply ask how she liked the trip. If she asks, "Have you ever been there?" you can compliment her on her choices, which you also enjoyed. Never get into a "mine is bigger than yours" type of discourse. TIAABB.

3. Remember that you are "valid" walking in. Don't seek approval. Don't try to indicate that you're eager to please or to conform. There is no one whose favor you need. I've had more than one executive lament, "I wish people would stop trying to curry my favor and simply point out where I'm wrong at times." He wasn't talking about subordinates; he was talking about his peers and suppliers.

4. You must engage in lifelong, sustainable learning. The world is changing too fast not to. That doesn't mean more degrees and useless certifications and initials after our names. It means reading the *Wall Street Journal* and the *New York Times* daily. It means keeping up with global developments, technology, sports, entertainment, law, politics, and demographics. We have to be truly educated daily, and we will be pretty much without peer if we are. (People who rely on the Internet, or worse, social media platforms, for news and learning are doing no safer than trying to improve themselves at the office water cooler's gossip mill.)

5. You need to look the part. The true mark of success is the impressiveness of even casual clothing. Your accessories should be smart and expensive, your shoes shined, your hair professionally cut. You should be dressed and groomed appropriately and well for the occasion. If you host or convey clients, you need a nice car.

This isn't about "dress for success," it's about your being happy with who you are and not afraid to look the part you should be playing.

Your personal journey from here is to embrace the lessons I've learned and use them for your own benefit. It's not merely about the content I've created but the *processes* by which and with which I've created my life.

EPILOGUE

The Liberal Artist

I've reflected in this book on the lessons I've learned that have helped me create the life I've led. Unlike executive biographies and celebrity hagiographies, this book concentrates on pragmatic, transferable skills and behaviors that are not unique to me or my circumstances. The effectiveness of my coaching and mentoring over the years has been in the power of other people adopting my techniques, not in trying to make them into me.

Judy Garland reflected once that she'd rather be an imperfect Judy Garland than a perfect someone else. Pablo Picasso told of his mother explaining that if he entered the military he'd be a great general, and if he entered the church he would be the pope. "Instead," he said, "I became a painter and wound up as Picasso."*

My life has been the compilation, absorption, and translation of others' experiences and learning. The dedication to this book includes my grammar school teachers, who started this process so magnificently. None is here to read this book, but all share in its content.

The fact is that I did experience some things that none of you

---

* As quoted in François Gilot and Carlton Lake, *Life with Picasso,* reprint edition (New York: Anchor, 1989).

(or precious few) could have, and it's difficult for me to represent them fully, but I'm going to try before I end this book. They are embedded in what was traditionally known as a liberal arts education. This education no longer exists, for all intents and purposes.

But let's start at the beginning. My grammar school, Hudson School, was a former cheese factory in the most densely populated city in the country at the time, Union City, New Jersey. During the winter we had to put rat poison in certain locations, because the rats apparently were still finding sufficient cheese or simply had created their own condominiums. One of my jobs was to pour ink from a giant spouted bottle into tiny inkwells in everyone's desk, where we would dip our straight pens. We learned to write in cursive script, which many educators want to eliminate today in favor of keyboard skills.

These teachers were feared and respected. Parents didn't argue with teachers, they took teachers' advice and disciplined their children. If you missed school, a truancy officer checked to see if the absence was legitimate. We didn't have "counselors" (which many teachers aspire to become today because it raises their pay grade and takes them out of the classroom). We had classes of fifteen to twenty pupils, separated into two groups per grade, one that scored better and performed better than the other. A student could move between the two groups, depending on grades.

I learned in English the eight parts of speech* and how to diagram a sentence. Those skills made me into a writer who became editor-in-chief of the high school newspaper and an award-winning editor-in-chief at Rutgers.

High school was largely a socialization experience, with bullies roaming the halls, and clearly two kinds of students: those applying to college and those not applying. The percentage was probably

---

* Noun, pronoun, verb, adverb, adjective, conjunction, preposition, interjection.

fifty–fifty at the time. There were no sexual harassment complaints, umbrage at prayers in school, refusals to recite the Pledge of Allegiance, or focuses on diversity. There was sex education, hormone-fed dating, and virtually no drugs. There *were* guidance counselors who were pretty hapless. Mine recommended a traditionally black college for my application, never realizing or checking the school beyond a listing, and gave me zero help in preparing for interviews.

I qualified to be interviewed at Columbia, but blew the session, totally unprepared. Rutgers happily accepted me, and on a combination of government loans (which I paid back, as did my wife, at Montclair University, in four years), merit scholarships, and part-time work, I paid the tuition. Rutgers is the state university of New Jersey, an original land-grant college, and at the time was a superb and richly diverse school. It was considered by many the "Ivy" of public universities.

And I enrolled in a liberal arts curriculum.

We didn't have to choose a major for two years, though I chose political science at the outset. We had to take sciences, language, and a slew of courses as *requirements*. Electives crept in as we moved to upper years.

Thus, I found myself taking courses in economic botany, animal reproduction, meteorology, oceanography, and geography. I did this to avoid chemistry and physics, which I knew loomed like the River Styx before me. I actually wound up with a minor in geology (with seventeen credits). I took psychology, sociology, economics, history, English literature, journalism, and constitutional law, along with myriad political science courses. I hunted for fossils in the Delaware Water Gap, tried to figure out intrusive sills in topographic diagrams, and learned about the alcoholic content of wines and beers. I nearly killed myself mastering French, since my high school Spanish courses failed me on the placement tests and I was forced to choose another language.

I've read Camus in French. Have you?

In our Western civilization course, our Swiss professor, with his Germanic accent, talked about "Louis Quatorze" and "*Le Roi Soleil*". A classmate lamented, "How am I going to pass this course when France had three kings at once, Louis XIV, Louis Quatorze, and a sun king?"

This liberal arts background does not exist anymore, nor does the discipline of grammar school, nor the forced socialization of high school that gained one street smarts. Back then we confronted our adversaries or figured out a way to deal with the problem; we didn't sue and parents weren't browbeating teachers.

We are surrounded today by people who don't know geography and can't understand history. They don't know where they are or where they came from. It's like being lost at sea with no sailing skills. I can tell you the capital of Senegal, and what was once its parent territory, French West Africa. Today, most people have trouble locating Kansas on an unmarked map or Laos on a marked map. They can't tell you the year of the War of 1812, and can't put in order the English, French, Russian, and American Revolutions.* In an age of instant access to data we have abandoned knowledge and forsaken wisdom. I am stunned by the lack of historical perspective we have, unless it's to bash someone using contemporary mores.

My advice to you is to compensate for the severe lack in our educational and socialization systems today. Five extracurricular activities, carpools, and coaching for SATs are not the answer to real learning. We are surrounded, indeed, by "Big Data," but we don't turn it into useful information when we need it.

You can't obtain your worldly information from the Internet, which is full of rumor, half-truths, and outright lies. You need to read original sources: histories, biographies, critical analyses. Don't

---

* I'm not telling you; look it up.

use revisionist history, which seeks to impose some of today's mores on a bygone world and push narrow political agendas. (Spanish invaders did not kill off indigenous peoples through disease, they were already declining at that time.*) Some of the greatest slave trade merchants were in the north, not the south, and Brown University is named after the worst family of all. (The university won't call a Christmas tree anything but a holiday tree, and doesn't recognize Columbus Day, but seems to feel being named after a slave-trading clan is okay, given the size of the original gift to the school.)

You need to read the *Wall Street Journal* for business acumen (and a wonderful arts section) and the *New York Times* for daily events (understanding the paper's left-wing bias). You must understand that the journalism of Edward R. Murrow, Walter Cronkite, and Huntley and Brinkley is long gone. Not long ago, television "journalist" Chris Matthews expressed that he felt it was his job to help create a successful presidency.† That's a long cry from exposing Joseph McCarthy and the House Un-American Activities Committee as bullies and frauds.

In my senior year at Rutgers I absolutely crushed the Legal Standard Aptitude Test (LSAT) and won a full scholarship to Rutgers Law, a top school. I recall everyone telling me forever that I should be a lawyer: "You debate well," "You can see facts quickly," "You are very persuasive." But that summer, I realized I didn't want to be a lawyer, working by the hour with clients on estates or divorces, or trying to climb the rungs in some corporate monolith.

When I visited the dean of admissions to tell her to give the scholarship to someone else (I always wonder who I funded), she

---

* See the books *1491* and *1493* by Charles C. Mann (New York: Knopf, 2005 and 2011, respectively).

† http://newsbusters.org/blogs/mark-finkelstein/2008/11/06/odd-job-matthews -says-his-role-make-obama-presidency-success

actually tried to grab my wrist across the desk to change my mind. I ran out of the room, down the steps, and into the streets of Newark as if the Four Horsemen of the Apocalypse were riding on my tail.

> **Mindsets:** There are a lot of dentists drilling on your teeth who don't want to be dentists, and a lot of therapists listening to your woes who are solely interested in curing their own.

I ran from "the law" as a maverick, not following others' advice, not wanting the conventional. I was armed with street smarts and a liberal arts education. As it turned out, that and a little talent were plenty.

Many of you, and your children, will never have street smarts because they aren't derived in SUVs, soccer practice, dance recitals, and computer camp. Virtually none of you will have the benefit of a liberal arts education, because it has been eliminated in reaction to political correctness (imagine studying Western civilization today), revisionist history, permissive curricula, and the tolerance of a five-year or more tenure in finishing undergraduate school. All of the vaunted home schooling, remote learning, and online universities have changed that not a whit.

My final advice to you here is this:

- Follow your own passion, no matter what people tell you. (I told both my kids in high school to pursue their passions. My daughter went to journalism school and became an executive producer, and my son went into a drama program, then on to an MFA, and is now a theater school president.)

- Surround yourself with liberal arts learning. Take on a second or third language. Travel the world, no matter how you have to scrimp or save to do so. Attend the theater. Become a polymath.

• Read voraciously: fiction, history, science, biographies, warfare, medicine, art, creativity, and so forth. Don't merely read people with whom you agree.

• Engage in writing. Use a personal journal, a blog, a newsletter; submit articles, op-ed pieces, letters to the editor; try fictional short stories and nonfiction based on your travels.

• Coach and teach others. There is no learning as profound as that which accrues when you teach and coach others what you think you already know!

I haven't been a maverick just to be different. I've been a maverick to be successful *on my own terms, not someone else's*. I don't ask or recommend that you pursue success on *my* terms, only that you recognize what success means to you and create your own path to that end.

That's living.

Appendix

The eleven reasons or causes for every corporate issue, in my experience and in no particular order:

1. Searching for blame instead of cause.
2. Failing to find cause before seeking a fix.
3. Making decisions without assessing risk.
4. Trying to form teams (and create "team building") when the groups are actually committees.
5. Failing to monitor performance or using poor evaluation methods.*
6. Confusing strategy with planning ("strategic planning" is an oxymoron).
7. Bouncing back and forth between strategy and tactics without realizing it.
8. Refusing to make tough decisions and exacerbating the problem.
9. Focusing on task and input instead of outcome and result.
10. Failing to listen adequately to customer feedback.
11. Missing the distinction between cause and effect, preventive action and contingent action.

---

* Essentially, people meet expectations, fail to meet expectations, or exceed expectations. That's it; anything else is superfluous.

References

Gilbert, Dan. *Stumbling on Happiness.* New York: Knopf, 2006.

Heinlein, Robert. *The Moon Is a Harsh Mistress.* New York: G. P. Putnam's Sons, 1964.

Kepner, Charles H., and Benjamin B. Tregoe. *The Rational Manager.* New York: McGraw-Hill, 1965.

Kübler-Ross, Elisabeth. *On Death and Dying.* New York: Macmillan, 1969.

Seligman, Martin. *Learned Optimism.* New York: Simon and Schuster, 2011.

Weiss, Alan. *The Great Big Book of Process Visuals.* East Greenwich, RI: Las Brisas Research Press, 2009.

Weiss, Alan. *Son of Process Visuals.* East Greenwich, RI: Las Brisas Research Press, 2011.

Weiss, Alan, and Richard Citrin. *The Resilience Advantage.* New York: Business Expert Press, 2016.

Weiss, Alan, with Mike Robert. *The Innovation Formula.* Cambridge: Ballinger (Harper & Row), 1988.

Weiss, Alan, and Kim Wilkerson. *The Language of Success.* New York: Business Expert Press, 2015.

Wheatley, Margaret. *Leadership and the New Science.* Oakland, CA: Berrett-Koehler, 2009.

Index